The Single Mother's Guide to Raising Remarkable Boys

D0169409

The
Single Mother's Guide to
RAISING REMARKABLE BOYS

GINA PANETTIERI WITH PHILIP S. HALL, PH.D.

Avon, Massachusetts

Published by
Adams Media, an F+W Publications Company
57 Littlefield Street, Avon, MA 02322. U.S.A.
www.adamsmedia.com

ISBN-13: 978-1-59869-440-6
ISBN-10: 1-59869-440-5

Printed in the United States of America.

J I H G F E D C B A

Library of Congress Cataloging-in-Publication Data
is available from the publisher.

This publication is designed to provide accurate and authoritative information
with regard to the subject matter covered. It is sold with the understanding
that the publisher is not engaged in rendering legal, accounting, or other
professional advice. If legal advice or other expert assistance is required, the
services of a competent professional person should be sought.
—From a *Declaration of Principles* jointly adopted by a Committee of the
American Bar Association and a Committee of Publishers and Associations

Many of the designations used by manufacturers and sellers to distinguish their
product are claimed as trademarks. Where those designations appear in this
book and Adams Media was aware of a trademark claim, the designations have
been printed with initial capital letters.

This book is available at quantity discounts for bulk purchases.
For information, please call 1-800-289-0963.

For my sons, Aric and Aaron. I'm so very proud of you both and of the men you have become.

For Michael, who got stuck in a snow bank in my driveway one snowy day in February 2001 and never really left. You provided a wonderful example to my herd of young men. You honestly believed in them and in this book. Their lives are changed for knowing you.

For Tim Lanfair and Jordan Church, both remarkable young men. It must have gotten too quiet in Heaven, so God called you home. You are deeply missed.

For Pat, Mike, and all the other boys who called my house "home," even briefly. I learned so much from all of you.

Finally, for Rachel, my daughter, who is, as a single mom, raising the next generation of remarkable young men in her sons, Danny and Aidan.

Never a dull moment.

ACKNOWLEDGMENTS

This book would not have been possible without the lessons learned from all the amazing males in my life, and all of the equally amazing moms who shared their stories and their advice with me. I appreciate all your time, effort, patience, and good humor.

This book, and our lives, also owe a great deal to my co-author, Dr. Phil Hall, who not only brought his immense knowledge and insight to this project, but also was extremely generous in offering his guidance and support to my family. I'm sure there were moments when I forgot to say "thank you" for the hour-long consultations and the action plans. Take this as a permanent standing "Thank you!"

I also tremendously appreciate the patience and perseverance of my editor, Paula Munier, and her assistant, Brendan O'Neill. I also want to thank Meredith O'Hayre and Heather Dubnick for keeping an eagle eye on the manuscript through the editing process.

I also owe a debt of gratitude to all the dedicated, gracious professionals who contributed their time and expertise to this project. Brette McWhorter Sember, J.D., former family law attorney and child law guardian, and Michael P. Devlin, corporate labor and employment attorney, both assisted with legal information related to single mom's issues. Dr. Karyn Purvis, director of Texas Christian University's Institute of Child Development, offered remarkable insights into the mind and communication style of young children. Corrie Lynne Player, parenting expert who raised more than forty children, both birth and foster (and can still laugh about it!), cheerfully elaborated on the many lessons she learned concerning creating a disciplined home environment.

Tim Barlett, Executive Director of the Bridgeport, Connecticut, YMCA, was extremely generous with his time, and his enthusiasm for a community-wide support network for children is contagious.

Laura Green, President and CEO of Nutmeg Big Brothers/ Big Sisters, likewise not only provided information, but also excitement and an amazing sense of what is possible when people give of themselves.

To all of you, and so many others who spoke with me, e-mailed me, sent me your own books, and shared your years of experience and knowledge, thank you so very much. This book was truly a group effort.

CONTENTS

Who Are We?

As a single mother of a boy, you've heard all the frightening statistics. No doubt, you've been told that "fatherless boys" are at a higher risk of juvenile delinquency, suffer poor academic and athletic performance, have higher incidences of drug and alcohol use, and run a greater likelihood of mental illness. Press releases from the Department of Health and Human Services warn that 63 percent of youth suicides are from fatherless homes. Of course, the media jumps onboard the panic bandwagon with sensationalistic stories predicting doom, peril, and chaos.

We've all read the headlines. Maggie Gallagher's *Newsweek* article screams "Fatherless Boys Grow Up into Dangerous Men," quoting a study by Cynthia Harper of the University of California and Sara McLanahan of Princeton University that concludes that boys without fathers are twice as likely to go to prison as boys from intact families. Charles Moore's report in the *Western Catholic Reporter* titled "Boys Lost in Fatherless Homes" adds to a single mom's guilt. The anti single-mom Web site *www .Dads4Kids.com* goes so far as to list "infamous fatherless people," including Charles Manson, Jeffrey Dahmer, and Jack the Ripper (though no one has ever conclusively determined who the Ripper actually was!). The Web site's message is clear, intimating that mothers who dare to attempt to raise boys on their own are creating crazed serial killers! It seems everywhere you turn, you're faced with some new negative report on the perils of single parenting, making it appear as if it is impossible for a single mother to successfully raise a boy. Don't believe it! We will show that it can be done, and we'll provide you with the tips and suggestions for doing it. But first, let's consider, why this growing attention on the issue of single moms raising sons?

According to a 2005 population report by the U.S. Census Bureau, there are 10.4 million single mothers raising children alone and more than 22 million children living in homes away from their fathers. In fact, there are more fatherless homes in the United States than anywhere else in the world, and the number continues to climb. At any given time, about a quarter of all American kids are living in a home headed by a single mother, and nearly one-third of all new births are to unmarried women. Over half of the kids born today will spend at least some time in a home without a father by the time they graduate high school. For the first time in history, married couples comprise a minority of American households, with a slight majority of households being headed up either by single parents or by unmarried adults living alone or in some sort of cohabitation arrangement. At the very least, then, by sheer force of numbers, what was once termed a "non-traditional" family unit of a single mother raising children is now quite commonplace, and single mother households are changing the face of the American family.

Given those numbers, and the negative public attention that the women raising boys alone issue has gotten in the media, one would imagine that society would be rushing to support these women. As Deborah Weinstein, director of the family income division of the Children's Defense Fund, explains, "If there's just one parent, it's far more difficult. We should support the single mom and help her as much as possible, rather than pointing the finger at her when it's another parent who isn't around, who hasn't been taking responsibility."

But that is not what is happening. Instead, many single mothers see themselves practically being criminalized by narrowly focused research and the media. While the few single fathers raising children are often considered candidates for sainthood and receive tremendous praise and accolades for such simple tasks as learning to make macaroni and cheese from a box or getting their child to school with matching socks, single mothers, in sharp contrast, find themselves in a no-win situation. If the mother strives to get ahead in her job, she's viewed as not putting her children first. If she takes an entry-level position to have more children-friendly hours, she's seen as unmotivated and shiftless. If she attempts to access government support programs to supplement her family's meager income, she's labeled a welfare mother, but if she goes to court to fight for unpaid child support owed by the child's father (and less than half of all court-ordered child support is ever collected by the family), so-called father's rights groups label her a money-grubbing parasite or worse!

The children of single mothers face negative labeling, as well. In a study by Paul Dawson of the perceptions of elementary school teachers, Dawson found many teachers automatically believe that a boy being raised by a single mother is more likely to be learning disabled, to have discipline problems, to be hyperactive, and to have serious, deep-seated emotional problems, even if he doesn't. This belief often becomes a dangerous self-fulfilling prophecy of poor performance, since the teacher is expecting the child to do poorly.

And while harmful and often erroneous assumptions and bias impact the sons of single mothers, single moms themselves face some very real challenges, including a greater risk of poverty, stress, loneliness, and isolation, and generally have less education and career status than women in two-parent families.

When all this slaps a single mother in the face, it can make her feel like throwing in the towel. Not only is it tough enough to enter a situation where the mother already feels overwhelmed and uncertain, but to then face criticism, scrutiny, and sometimes even scorn is like trying to learn to walk a tightrope that's already on fire!

But why this societal rush to blame single mothers? Nancy Dowd, author of *In Defense of Single Parent Families* and *Redefining Fatherhood*, believes she knows why. "Imagine," she writes, "if all these mother-headed families were successful. Think about what that would mean. It would mean that men aren't essential. Suppose that women didn't need men in terms of economics, that they would raise healthy children without men being present in the household. That seems very threatening and very dangerous." In a society where women are gaining in all respects on previous male bastions of power, with young women earning the majority of professional degrees and even taking a slight (and ever growing) majority in admissions to medical school and law school, and increasingly becoming the chief executive officers of major corporations, women are being viewed with increasing jealousy and suspicion by some men. If women were now to be viewed as perfectly adequate to successfully raise children, even male children, entirely on their own, where does that leave men? As noted by Louise Silverstein, professor of psychology at Yeshiva University and co-founder of the Yeshiva Fatherhood Project, "Never underestimate the power of misogyny in male-dominant society." Is it possible that the mom-bashing statistics aren't presenting the whole picture?

> "When people ask me who was his role model, it drives me mad. I was his role model!"
>
> *Kelly Armstrong, mother of pro cyclist, Lance Armstrong*

While the most attention-grabbing headlines have taken a negative view of single mothers raising boys, there's a growing body of research that contradicts the commonly held beliefs regarding fatherless boys and single parent households. Studies performed at the Ohio State University by Douglas Downey, James Ainsworth-Darnell, and Mikaela Dufur have refuted the theory that children from single mother households are disadvantaged because the lack the presence of a father, and instead focus on issues of income and other socioeconomic advantages as the real culprit behind differences in performance between children from single mother households and those from "traditional" families.

A second study at Cornell University, by researcher Henry Riccuitti, has concluded that single parenting does not appear to have a negative effect on the behavior or educational performance of the mother's children. Instead, Riccuitti stresses that it's the mother's ability and her attitude that are the pivotal factors in the children's success. Riccuitti even goes so far as to conjecture that there are advantages to single mother households because of generally smaller family size and the increased likelihood of the presences of maternal grandparents, aunts, uncles, and others in the household, sometimes allowing for even more individual attention for the child from many adults.

"I know many single mothers who have raised wonderful sons, who are now incredible adults. Love, boundaries and limits, appropriate expectations, and a strong support system are the most important factors."

Jamie, single mother of one son

Instead of forecasting a future of difficulties, these researchers are concluding that, given the proper support, parenting skills, and resources, single mothers are not only just as successful at raising outstanding young men as their married counterparts, but they may actually also have a number of advantages.

"I found that raising Adam alone was actually a positive experience for both of us. Our relationship has gotten much closer. We have time to talk more, and without the stress of an unhappy marriage, he's a much happier child."

Carol, registered nurse and mother of two

An article titled "Education for the Twenty-First Century," published in the April 19, 2000, edition of *Education Week*, reported that the time fathers spend interacting with their children is less than 5 minutes a day by the time children are adolescents. If this is true, where is the quality "fathering" so many experts insist is essential to a boy's healthy development? Are boys being raised by single moms really missing out on all that much? Is there actually anything a father provides that a mother cannot? Can a mother by herself really raise a male child to be just as successful as a two-parent family could? Consider this list of men raised by single moms:

- **Lance Armstrong:** pro cyclist and seven-time winner of the Tour de France. Founder of the Lance Armstrong Foundation (a cancer support and education group)
- **Ed Bradley:** late CBS TV news correspondent and co-editor of *60 Minutes*
- **Les Brown:** best-selling author and motivational speaker
- **Dr. Benjamin Carson:** director of the Division of Pediatric Neurosurgery at Johns Hopkins and author of three best-selling books
- **Bill Clinton:** forty-second president of the United States and former governor of Arkansas
- **Bill Cosby:** actor, comedian, activist, author, winner of the Bob Hope Humanitarian Award
- **Tom Cruise:** actor, producer

- **James Garfield:** major general of the Union army, college president, twentieth president of the United States
- **Alan Greenspan:** chairman of the Federal Reserve from 1987–2006, Winner of the Presidential Medal of Freedom
- **Alexander Haig:** former White House chief of staff and secretary of state
- **Henry Hazlitt:** famed author and economist
- **Rickey Henderson:** 1990 American League MVP, baseball's most prolific run scorer
- **J. R. Moehringer:** winner of the 2000 Pulitzer Prize for feature writing, best-selling author of *The Tender Bar,* his memoir of his fatherless youth and tribute to his mother's courage and strength.
- **Barack Obama:** senator from Illinois, civil rights attorney
- **Quentin Tarantino:** film director, actor, Oscar-winning screen writer
- **Bill Weir:** co-anchor of *Good Morning America Weekend Edition* and four-time Emmy winner

Whether through divorce, the death of the father, or the mother's decision to have a child without a father in the picture, nearly 11 million families in America are currently headed by a single mother. Even in families where the father initially visits with the children and remains involved in their lives shortly after divorce, the father's presence usually diminishes greatly over time. Within ten years of divorce, more than two-thirds of children report not having seen their father within the last year. America isn't suffering from an epidemic of single mothers. It's experiencing the mass disappearance of its fathers.

Raising boys is always a challenge. Even in "intact" homes, boys encounter far more difficulties growing up than do their female counterparts. The Pell Institute for the Study of Opportunity in Higher Education reports that boys are more likely to suffer from learning disabilities, with a staggering three-quarters of learning disabled students being males. They're brought in for treatment and evaluation of attention deficit disorder (ADD) six times more frequently than girls. And according to the Centers for Disease Control, they're more likely to die in accidents, and males commit suicide more often. In fact, 86 percent of suicides occur with boys.

> "Basically, once we were divorced, my ex lost interest in the children. I would plead and cajole him to call or visit them, but he was too busy with his new life. The boys definitely felt abandoned and rejected. I don't think any of the issues they had right after the divorce had to do with me being a single mom, but with what their father had done to them. They were very angry little boys."
>
> *Rachel, mother of two*

Boys also suffer in a divorce much more than girls do, though studies seem to indicate that this is due much more to the stress within the household prior to the divorce than any actual changes in lifestyle afterward. So is it any wonder why boys present unique challenges, particularly in the first few years following a divorce?

The truth is that being a single mother is not all gloom and doom. Let's look at some heartening facts and figures. Recent studies have also concluded that, though divorce can be a time of upheaval and emotional turmoil, the vast majority of children rebound well within just a few years of the event, and that, as noted above, the problems associated with the sons of single mothers are much more related to the stress and conflict that led up to the divorce, rather than the child's new lifestyle. A 2002 report by E. Mavis Hetherington and John Kelly, entitled "For Better or for Worse: Divorce Reconsidered," compared divorced families with non-divorced families, found that children in non-divorced, high-conflict homes turned out to have similar problems as children of divorce, and concluded that these children would have had the same problems whether their parents had divorced or not. In fact, for children whose parents were in conflict while married, the new, stable, single parent home after divorce was a relief and not nearly as traumatic.

In fact, in a study by Serge Saintonge on the support group, Big Brothers of America, boys from single mother homes who had the benefit of the Big Brothers group actually scored lower on the Feelings of Parental Rejection Test than did boys from "intact families," and other tests showed these "Little Brother" boys to have good self-esteem, lower levels of depression, and less incidence of delinquency. Saintonge's findings indicate the feelings of rejection many boys experience was not due to abandonment as much as it is parental conflict. The study also bode well for those boys from single mother homes whose mothers recognized the usefulness of seeking active and engaged male role models for their fatherless sons. These boys' futures looked bright.

"I didn't feel I had a choice in becoming a single mother. My children's father was acting in ways that damaged my sons emotionally and simply wouldn't change or get counseling. The children's school counselor actually labeled their father "corrosive." Something had to be done."

Anne, professional services, mother of three

My Own Background as a Single Mother of Boys
I became a single mother of two boys, my sons Aaron and Aric, in the late 1990s, when their father and I separated and ultimately divorced. The children had not had a great deal of contact with their father for several years leading up to the divorce, so the change was not as abrupt or dramatic as many families encounter,

and my career allowed me to work from home offices, so there was little disruption in the daily lives of the children. I was almost always available if someone needed to talk, and the kids were nearly never alone at home. Despite this seemingly ideal set of circumstances, we still went through some very rough patches. Both boys were confused and hurt by the nearly complete absence of their father from their lives following the divorce, and their feelings of rejection and abandonment resulted in periods of depression and anxiety. I often felt at a loss as to how to communicate with them. They didn't respond to the same approaches as had worked for my older, adult daughter, Rachel. Questions regarding how they were or how their day went were usually met with vague replies of "okay," "fine," or "whatever." It seemed some special secret handshake was needed to get my boys to say more than two words to me. But I also realized their withdrawal and silence combined with what was clearly depression was a dangerous mixture and I had to find a way to break through.

I quickly learned that I could not force them into face-to-face dialogues. Asking them direct questions got me nothing but guarded looks and meaningless reassurances. Fortunately, I quickly stumbled into the boy gold mine of communication, the car trip. While both kids would clam up and avoid eye contact if they were cornered into a discussion, side-by-side in a car while I drove them to work, school, or activities allowed them the opportunity to talk without the stress of eye contact. In fact, it turned out, my boys are very typical in that while it's nearly impossible to get a direct answer out of them looking them in the eye, they will often become veritable motor mouths while they're engaged in some other activity.

Since we lived in a rural mountain town in Northwestern Connecticut, it was a long drive to anywhere, a blessing in disguise as it turned out. A trip to the mall or a ride to a concert arena or ski mountain often signaled my sons to launch into lengthy stories about the troubles friends were having, what was going on at school, or simply discussions of what kinds of cars they wanted. By quietly listening and only occasionally prompting with a guiding question, I learned to allow the boys to tell me at their own pace what was going on in their lives, and from there, we could work on healing.

Our home also quickly became an informal halfway house for other fatherless teens in our community. Extremely gregarious and entertaining, my sons gathered a large and varied collection of friends, and they wouldn't hesitate to bring home a new "brother." While far from luxurious, our house had a bit of extra room, and the boys were always willing to share whatever space they had. Since I worked from home, and was nearly always home to supervise, other mothers felt comfortable allowing their boys to move in, or at the very least, spend lots of time at our house. Some boys joined us while their own families were temporarily having problems, others came when their own mothers needed a bit of a respite in order to get their own lives in order, and some came so that they could remain in the same school while their families were relocating frequently. We often had anywhere from two to four extra boys living in our home, and while the result was often noisy and a bit chaotic (not to mention the challenges of cooking for a herd of teenage males), the boys provided an amazing support network for each other. They tutored each other in school subjects, protected each other from bullies, and spent long hours talking about their problems. Loneliness and isolation was never an issue, for any of us, and the boys were not only there for each other, they were there for me, too. It was a unique experience that I hope to share with you in many ways through the pages of this book. As a group, they taught me a great deal about what it is to grow up male in America, and showed me that given time, love, and compassion, fatherless boys can, indeed, grow up into marvelous men.

My Co-Author's Background as a Child Psychologist—Phil Hall

As a licensed psychologist with thirty-four years of experience, it has been my lifelong work to help children in times of stress. For several decades, I served fourteen different school districts covering nearly half of South Dakota. During that time, I also served as a consultant to the State of South Dakota with the assignment of working with children that schools were struggling to adequately serve. Later, I was the Director of Psychological Services for the University of South Dakota Medical School Clinic. I have also served as the Director of the School Psychology Training Program at the University of South Dakota and at Minot State University. While at Minot State University, I started and directed a clinic for oppositional children and their families.

From this work, I learned many important things about children and about parenting. The most important thing that I learned about children is that they want to fit in. They want to belong. They want to learn what it takes to get along with others and to become an adult. When they struggle, it is not for lack of caring or wanting, it's for a lack of knowing how. With regard to parenting, I learned that children need to be valued, always and regardless. Indeed, children will not be and cannot be successful unless someone values them. Second, I learned that parents can best help their children by providing the necessary structure and support children need to grow and to learn.

In my mind's eye, I can see hundreds and hundreds of such children. Alex is one of them. Alex's parents divorced when he was ten years old. When I saw him eight years later, he was still struggling.

Alex's first words to me were memorable. "You're a shrink, aren't you?" Before I could answer, he said, "I eat shrinks for lunch. They come in two flavors. There are the shrinks they send out to get me to behave, and then there are the shrinks that think all of my problems relate back to bad toilet training or some other early childhood experience that I can't even remember. What kind of shrink are you?"

"I am the newest flavor of shrink, Alex," I said, "I simply want to help you."

"Help me. How? I don't have any problems!"

"Well, I see two problems," I told him. "One is that you seldom make it through an entire day of school without getting kicked out of one class or another. The other problem is that in spite of being bright and capable, you have been in high school three years now and you haven't earned enough credits to be a freshman. At this rate, you will be thirty-two years old before you graduate from high school. So if that isn't your goal, I restate my original question. How can I help you? Tell me what it is that you'd like to be doing three years from now, and I will do everything in my power to help you get there."

"You'd really do that?" he asked.

"I will."

In a nutshell, that is what I can contribute to this book. I will give you, the single parent of a boy, the tools and understandings to help your child through his difficult times.

Let's get started!

As Moms of Remarkable Boys, you are

- From all walks of life, from teenage moms in school to mature women in their fifties raising son by adoption;
- from all socioeconomic backgrounds from working class to upper class;
- from every ethnic and religious background;
- living alone with your children, or with family members, friends, or a life partner; and
- the new face of America. The future is what you make it.

CHAPTER 1

Taking Inventory

Headlights splashed across the window, and I was already heading to the front door. It was starting to get late and I had been expecting my then fourteen-year-old son, Aric, to call at any moment for a ride home. He'd gone to visit friends and when a car pulled in, I'd assumed he caught a ride home with someone else's parents. So I was completely unprepared to find a police cruiser sitting in front of my door. Fear and confusion turned to something else when I saw my son climbing out of the back seat. The officer turned him toward my door with a hand on his shoulder and my son hung his head, avoiding eye contact. I had unconsciously assumed The Stance. As the mother of a son, you no doubt know The Stance. Arms crossed angrily across my chest, foot tapping, eyes narrowed. I had no idea what had happened, but I knew it wasn't good.

The officer took one look at my face and summed it up. "I guess I don't have to ask if this one's yours."

"He's mine, all right," I assured him.

The policeman gently urged my son through the door. "Aric, why don't you head on in while I talk privately with your mom?"

I was too confused and bewildered to even speak. My mind was racing as I considered all the possibilities.

"Your son and a few other boys were picked up on Route 309, riding in an improper vehicle," the officer explained.

"Like a stolen car?" I felt faint.

"No, ma'am," the policeman countered quickly. Then he seemed to hesitate. "A hay wagon."

All I could do was blink.

"A hay wagon, towed behind a tractor."

My hands made odd circles in the air, begging some kind of explanation.

The officer pushed his hat back on his head and rubbed the back of his neck. "Well, I came up on the boys stalled out in the road. They'd decided they were going to head over to Simsbury, and they'd been using this tractor to pull the wagon for quite some time, and the tractor had just given up the ghost." He shook his head, amazed. "They'd rigged up the wagon with garden benches for seats, and had rope tied to the benches for seat belts. They even had flashlights with red tape across the lenses tied to either end of the back side of the wagon to use as 'brake lights.'"

I pondered this for a moment. "Fairly creative," I finally had to concede.

"I thought so," the office agreed. "Anyway, I'm sure you realize it's not legal to use that sort of vehicle for transporting passengers on a public road. Could be downright dangerous. By the time I found them, though, they weren't going anywhere fast."

"So what happens now?" I asked. "Do the boys have to have a court appearance or something?"

The policeman shook his head, again, grinning crookedly. "No, no, they've already learned their lesson. As I said, the tractor clunked out, so I made them push the whole rig all the way back to where they started. I drove behind with my flashers on. It was a long, slow march. Anyway, that's pretty much the end of it." He hesitated a moment. "Don't be too hard on him. I remember being a boy like that myself." He turned and headed back to his car as I turned toward the house.

My son was waiting for me at the kitchen table, looking like he was awaiting the executioner.

I sat down opposite him. "Well?"

My son began a rapid-fire explanation. "We couldn't get a ride!" he protested. "We asked Adam's father, but he was too busy, and then Adam said, hey, there's the tractor, I know how to drive that, and we can fix up the hay wagon so everyone can ride in it . . ."

"*Adam?*" I cut in. "You listened to *Adam?*" This was a boy who had tried to ride a mattress off the roof of his house.

My son shrugged as if he'd been helpless against a force of nature.

"Do you realize how dangerous that was?" My voice was rising to a pitch heard only by dogs and certain kinds of insects. "If a car had come around a bend too fast, it could have hit all of you!"

"Tractors are on the road up there all the time," he countered, accurately.

"That's not the point and you know it! And what were you doing on Route 309, anyway?"

My son was trapped. No way out. "We were going to Simsbury to try to meet girls."

I laid my head down on the table. I could picture the whole thing. They were thinking they were going to roll into town in a hay wagon decked out with garden benches with rope seat belts and just wow the local females. My shoulders started quaking and I started drumming the table with one clenched fist.

"Mom," my son started nervously. "Mom, don't get upset. Nobody got hurt."

I couldn't keep it in any longer. I burst out laughing, slapping the table. The more I thought, the harder I laughed. I caught my son's bewildered face and nearly rolled on the floor. I wiped my streaming eyes and thought one word.

"*Boys!*"

Understanding the Boy's Brain

Let's face it: boys are very different from girls. They think things, say things, and do things that would be completely alien to a female. If your kid is up on the garage roof with a cape made out of a bath towel, testing the reality of gravity, chances are it's your son and not your daughter. And the child who leaps feet first onto your stomach while you're napping probably also has a Y chromosome. The baby who mysteriously decides it's hysterical to repeatedly head-butt the wall until you're worried you'll have to keep him in a helmet until he leaves for college? Again, likely wearing a diaper with all the padding up front.

Then again, it's more often a boy who'll sit for hours taking apart the family's prized heirloom clock, only to then reassemble it perfectly.

Boys are wonderful, sensitive, creative, loyal, and loving. They're also complex, challenging, active, and impulsive. And one thing you know as the single mother of a boy is they're different from you, in so many ways.

For decades, the nature versus nurture controversy raged on regarding gender and behavior. Are boys the way they are because they were born that way, or are they socialized into a set of behaviors our culture defined as "male"? In the infamous Baby X case, people were handed a baby who was identified as either a boy or a girl and told to play with the baby any way they wished. When the subjects thought they were playing with a boy, they offered him trucks and balls. When the baby had been identified as a girl, the subjects offered her a doll. Trouble is, it was always the same baby! So how much of what a boy becomes is due to what he's born with, and how much to what he's taught?

New technologies like MRI (magnetic resonance imaging) and PET (positron emission tomography) have allowed scientists and researchers to look at the differences between boys' brains and girls' brains in entirely new and different ways, and to reflect on how the differences they've discovered impact how the genders think, feel, and behave.

On average, an adolescent boy's corpus callosum (which connects the two hemispheres of the brain) is about one-quarter smaller than a girl's. This probably means that there's more communication between those hemispheres in a girl's brain. As you no doubt know, the left hemisphere of the brain is the part that's logical, sequential, and analytical, while the right hemisphere controls random thought, synthesizing, and holistic thought. Actually, some experts believe that what females sometimes call "intuition" is really the effective communication between the emotional and the logical, reasoning hemispheres of the brain. This may also explain why boys seem to have more difficulty in discerning a wide and subtle range of emotions in other people.

Boys also have weaker neural connectors in the temporal lobe region. These connectors are associated with listening skills, detecting cues by tone of voice, and detailed memory storage, and since the female brain has stronger connectors, these skills in females are more acute than in males. Again, this could lead to males seeming to have more difficulty in perceiving a range of emotions from cues.

In another memory storage area of the brain, again, girls seem to be at the advantage. Female brains have a larger hippocampus, which particularly influences language skills, possibly explaining why females are more verbally adept as children and may speak earlier and more frequently. Girls use language much more often and more fluently as children to communicate with and interpret their world, while boys are much more hands on, learning better through manipulation.

Boys and girls also appear to use the cortical area of their brains differently. By using tests to determine which part of the brain manages different kinds of tasks, researchers have found that girls use more of the cortical area of their brains for tasks involving speaking and emotion. Boys use more of the cortical area for spatial and mechanical tasks. This explains a boy's natural attraction for taking things apart and (hopefully) putting them back together, and their relative ease when tackling spatial relations tasks. Boys have an easier time grasping mechanical concepts, while females process language and emotional cues with greater facility. And it's more than just what comes easily to the different genders. Stimulation of the cortical area is, in a way, experienced as pleasure, and it drives the two sexes toward activities that are most stimulating and rewarding for them. Studies have also shown that most boys *experience* words and feelings differently than girls.

The prefrontal cortex of boys is less active than that of girls, and develops at a later age. The prefrontal cortex is part of the brain that plays the executive role. When an impulse or thought comes to the prefrontal cortex, that part of the brain examines what might be the consequence of carrying out the impulse. If, upon consideration, it seems like the impulse or idea should be carried out, the prefrontal cortex formulates a plan of action. This less-developed prefrontal cortex of young boys explains the "act now, think later" impulsive behavior typical of boys. Additionally, boys have less serotonin in their blood and brain, which has also been linked to increased impulsive behavior. Boys also have less oxytocin, which, again, makes them more impulsive and less able to sit quietly and calmly. Is it no wonder that boys sometimes seem a bundle of restless energy, particularly if called upon to remain still for long periods?

There are even differences attributable to the level of testosterone in the amniotic fluid before birth. Babies, both male and female, when exposed to higher levels of testosterone in the uterus, scored higher on so-called male attributes like spatial relations. They were also stronger athletes, since they had better heart and lung development. However, they had poorer scores on interpersonal skills. The most interesting aspect was the influence the hormone had within the genders. Some of the highest-testosterone females scored as well as the average male on spatial relations tests! All this goes to say that though there are differences between the genders, there are differences from one boy to the next. Each child is unique, possessed of a special, individual set of traits, and some of these will be influenced even before he's born!

Can You Hear Me Now? How Males Hear Differently

There's even medical evidence that boys *hear* differently than girls. Beginning in the late 1950s, Professor John Corso of Penn State University performed a systemic study of the hearing of boys and girls. He showed that girls hear better than boys do, especially in the range of normal speech tones. Other studies supported Corso's findings. A report by Martti Sorri and P. Rantakallio in *Scandinavian Audiology* reported that hearing impairment is about 70 percent more common in teenage boys than in teenage girls.

A study by Hiroaki Sato revealed differences in the structure of the inner ear. Girls are born with a cochlea that is shorter and stiffer, showing a physical reason behind girls' more sensitive hearing. So what does this mean for boys?

"I wasn't aware of the hearing differences between boys and girls, but I learned early on that if I wanted to get my son's attention, I needed to speak in a deeper, somewhat louder voice. At first I thought it was just that the deeper voice sounded more authoritative, so he paid attention when I used it. Now I realize it might be that he can just hear me more clearly when I use it! My friends actually tease me about knowing when I'm speaking with my son on the phone because I immediately use my 'boy voice.'"

Anne, mother of two

Consider a parent's primary mode of communication—speech. Furthermore, consider what it means that boys' hearing is particularly less sensitive in the higher frequencies and softer volumes usually associated with female speech. Do you sometimes feel like you're talking to yourself when trying to address your child? Perhaps, in a way, you are!

Couple the boy's natural difficulties in discerning higher frequencies with the fact that most teachers in elementary education are female. Is your son not paying attention, or is he simply having trouble making out what the teacher is saying? Imagine sitting a few rows back in a classroom, not clearly hearing what's going on at the front of the class. How difficult would it be to remain attentive and not allow one's imagination to wander or become restless and bored?

Males not only have a more difficult time hearing, they're also far less likely than females to realize that they're having difficulty. A Danish study reported in the *British Journal of Audiology* demonstrated that males seem unaware of their hearing problems. So, even if your son is having difficulty hearing or understanding at times, it's unlikely he even realizes it and will probably reply negatively if you ask him about it. Women often accuse males of having selective hearing, since they seem able to block out things they don't want to hear or don't feel like responding to. Part of this might be a natural male tendency to not feel the same social pressure to respond that females seem to feel, but another factor may be that if they're not cued up to pay close attention, males may simply not hear you!

Whereas there are striking anatomical differences between the brains of boys and girls, there are also subtle but important differences between the brains and processing abilities.

As we'll explore later on in this book, all these differences greatly influence how your son experiences and interacts with his world. It also means that as the mother of a boy, you need to be aware of his different way of communicating, his different need for physical activity, and the unique way he learns. Beyond that, it's important to respect and express your appreciation for his very maleness.

Too often, both at home and in school, boys' behavior and abilities are judged relative to a standard of female behavior and abilities. Boys who cannot sit still quietly and focus as long as females can are thought to be hyperactive. Boys' natural aggressiveness is often frowned upon. A boy's slower verbal development is considered cause for concern, while his prowess with spatial relations is overlooked. It's the original case of trying to fit a square peg into a round hole. Instead, we need to strive to embrace boys for who they are, and at the same time, to fight stereotypes of males that limit our sons' horizons.

Knowing What You Don't Know, and Appreciating What You Do!

Raising boys as a single mom can feel overwhelming at times. There's never enough time, never enough money, never enough help, never enough you! Or at least it feels that way. There will probably be moments when you'll be completely bewildered, exhausted, and utterly depleted. Then, suddenly, out of the blue, some small, wonderful thing happens, as simple as an unexpected hug or kiss, and you realize all over again that you wouldn't trade your life for anything in the world. Take a moment to think of all you do know, and be thankful for the gifts you've been given. It's most important during those moments when you feel absolutely frazzled to remind yourself you're doing better than you realize!

In a recent poll by ABC news and *Good Housekeeping* magazine, moms were asked to rank their relationships and their laments. All the moms responding rated their relationships with their kids as "good" or "excellent," with nearly 70 percent reporting an excellent relationship. Working moms reported no more guilt issue than did stay-at-home moms. Working moms were confident of their parenting skills, and most simply wished they had more time with their children (a problem we tackle later on in Chapter 8). Single moms felt as strongly about their parenting skills and their relationships with their children as did moms with partners. Moms today are aware, focused, and deeply involved with their families. They're proactive in addressing their children's problems, and have learned to advocate aggressively for their children's needs. The fact you're reading this book shows you're a mom who'll head off problems at the pass, and face those that arise with strength and self-assurance.

> "Your primary obligation is your child's welfare and needs. Your child must come first in your life. Once that is established, the rest will come naturally. Don't worry about needing to do something special because you have sons. They will develop normally even if you don't play baseball with them. Boys are a lot of fun!"
>
> *Deborah, single mom of two sons*

Constructing an Action Plan

As you work through this book, you'll be introduced to a number of concepts, tips, and practices drawn from researchers, teachers, and moms raising boys without fathers. Some will be useful to you at the stage of life your son is in right now, and others will prepare you for what is yet to come. To make the best use of the information, take a few moments now to think about and identify your own main areas of concerns.

As a single mom raising a son, you may be concerned that

- Your son feels rejected or abandoned;
- Your son will be a higher risk of using drugs;

- Your son will lack a male role model and will grow up less masculine;
- Your son will be more likely to be homosexual;
- Your son will be depressed, hurt, and angry; or
- Your son will suffer academically.

As the mom, you may be concerned for yourself that you

- Don't know how to raise boys to be good men,
- Don't understand what boys go through during puberty,
- Don't like or understand the things boys like, and
- Don't know how to communicate with boys.

Now take a few minutes to list in the spaces below your own concerns about raising your son in home without a father present. Be as honest as you can. You don't need to share this list with anyone, so you don't have to worry about how it will look to anyone else. Don't worry about appearing insecure, or that your concerns seem either silly or insurmountable, and don't be afraid to confront concerns that are uncomfortable to think or talk about. In the pages ahead, you'll be meeting other moms who confronted those same issues, and you'll be reading about extensive research into the problems single moms face, with both surprising and reassuring results.

My concerns for my son:

_____

_____

_____

_____

_____

My concerns for myself as a single mother of a son:

_____

_____

_____

_____

_____

As a Mom of a Remarkable Boy, you

- Understand that there are fundamental differences between boys and girls;
- Strive for understanding, acceptance, and compassion; and
- Are willing to look inside and face your concerns for your son, and yourself, and then take action!

CHAPTER 2

Early Childhood and the Fatherless Boy

For the very youngest of children, the absence of a father in the house can often be handled very successfully, whether due to the abrupt departure of the dad caused by divorce, or because there was a carefully thought-out decision to affirmatively enter into motherhood as a non-traditional family, or simply because motherhood just happened.

Until the age of three, a child's world is centered quite strongly on the mother. She has, since birth, been the source of warmth, comfort, nourishment, and security. She's been playmate, teacher, nurse, and protector. Even in traditional two-parent households, an infant or toddler is often unhappy being left with anyone other than mom, even if the father has been a constant familiar presence.

However, says Dr. Karyn Purvis, Director of the Texas Christian University's Institute of Child Development, a child can encode a male presence even if it's not the father, and that that process is very beneficial to a boy. Encoding is the term psychologists use to refer to the process by which a mental representation is formed in the memory, in this case, the child's understanding of "male." This encoding of a male presence is vitally important to a child's later self-awareness, she believes, and so she encourages single mothers to have other males around the child on a regular basis, whether it's grandfathers, uncles, or close family friends. "It's a protective factor," she says, "that's normally served by the father. In my estimation, there's a sleeper effect in the early years so that even if a child doesn't show interest in a male figure, a male presence is still important. I think there's a protective factor in having that presence to encode."

Recent Loss of the Father

In the case of divorce or separation, a child under the age of three really doesn't understand much regarding the change the family is going through. However, your son can probably sense, and react to, whatever stress, grief, and anger you may be experiencing. He can certainly sense that his mother is upset, and that she has withdrawn from him emotionally while she's dealing with the situation, and this can cause him insecurity and stress. It's vital to try to continue on as normally as possible, for your own sake as well as your son's. It's natural to feel overwhelmed during this period, especially with a young child to care for, and you may find yourself depressed, resentful, and confused. You may even find yourself at times feeling that it's unfair that your baby's father is out having fun (or so it seems) while you're home working twice as hard to raise your child alone. It's important that you seek counseling and support for yourself. Taking care of yourself is the only way you'll be able to care for your child. This topic is treated in detail in Chapter 14.

The most important thing you have to provide your son with now at this stage is emotional security. Continue to snuggle and cuddle your child. Long, leisurely story times and lots of one-on-one time are important. For your youngster, just having you there and involved in the most important thing. Try to keep his surroundings as familiar as possible and disrupt his life as little as you can. Don't make unnecessary changes to his physical environment. Even if you're tempted to completely redo your entire apartment, temper your impulses for a while. Too many changes, too quickly, can create a feeling of insecurity in your son.

DR. HALL ON A TODDLER'S WORLD

A newborn does not make a clear distinction between himself and mom. However, by six months, the infant is starting to realize that there are two people in the relationship. But in his mind, he is the important one. For a toddler, getting his needs met are paramount: being fed; having a sticky, wet diaper changed; not being too hot or too cold; and being held and comforted by a nurturing caregiver. A single mother can readily meet these needs. The toddler does not fret about a dad, worry about his gender identity, or wonder what he is going to be when he grows up.

If circumstances dictate that you need to return to work outside the home when you had previously been a stay-at-home or work-from-home mom, and your child is not accustomed to day care, try to provide for child care in your own home, at least for a while, whether through a family member or a paid sitter. Staying in familiar surroundings, and not having to cope with too many new situations at once, will help your child feel secure. Children under the age of three really don't require the constant socialization with other children a day-care environment presents, so don't feel you'd be depriving your child by providing care in his own home. Children this age tend to play more side by side than interacting and are quite content with adult companionship.

No matter what the family background, some things are universal. Playing with your child, interacting with him closely, looking into his eyes, and speaking with him will help develop his sense of self-esteem. Again, simply your presence close by and nurturing is the most important thing, and exactly what you do is secondary. Your young son likely has very little concept of being male and will likely engage in play that's less gender-specific, so don't feel you have to encourage more masculine activities in order to compensate for the lack of a father or to explore your son's male interests at this age. While he may prefer trucks to dolls, he's just as likely to be amused by trying on mom's hats or carrying her purse, and he may choose a ballerina's tutu or a princess gown as a costume as readily as a cowboy hat and six-guns. He's only just beginning to be able to identify males from females based on their appearances, and is parroting what he's been told when he calls himself a boy, without any real idea of what that exactly mean. Playing at this age with "girl toys" or expressing an interest in clothes, stories, or activities normally associated with females is no way an indication that your son isn't masculine enough or is going to grow up effeminate.

There's a vast difference between gender identification and gender conformity. Boys will develop a sense of being a boy quite naturally. Fathers tend to enforce gender roles much more strongly than mothers do, and they tend to express alarm at what they perceive as inappropriate preferences in clothes, toys, or behavior. By contrast, while a mother in a fatherless household may worry that she won't be able to raise her son to be masculine enough, she has the advantage that she's not fighting to overcome restrictive thinking forced upon her son by a reactionary, threatened male.

The Preschool Boy, Ages Three Through Six

A boy who is somewhat older will experience the absence of his father quite a bit differently, particularly if he'd developed a close relationship with his father or the departure is very abrupt. A child this age is quite aware of things going on around him, and tends to think himself to be the cause of anything that happens.

Guilt, Confusion, and Fear: Helping Your Son Adjust

Preschool children have the ability for magical thinking, which is to say that they often think that what they thought or did influenced some event in their larger world. So, they might also be likely to view themselves as the cause for their father's departure, feeling that they must have done something bad for Daddy to have left them. They might also wonder that if Daddy is no longer with Mom, then will he stop loving them next? They often feel abandoned and fearful. They may cry for Daddy to stay with them at the end of visitation, promising that they'll be good if only Daddy won't leave again. As Mom, this scene can simply tear your heart out.

IF SO, SOLVE IT—HANDLING VISITATION: NOTES FROM DR. HALL

During parenting, your child will have behavior problems that have a way of happening again and again. When they do, the adage "Happen once, shame on you. Happen twice, shame on me," applies. Tearful, emotion-laden separations when Dad departs after a visit are a case in point. There are some simple things you can do to make those inevitable separations less traumatic for everyone. For starters, at the outset of the visit, let the child know when Dad will be coming back for his next visit. Dad should help the child circle this date on the calendar. Second, it needs to be stated how long Dad will be staying for this visit. Dad should assist the child in setting this pre-announced departure time on an alarm clock. When the alarm clock rings, Dad asks, "What does that ringing mean?" The child will know the answer, and they can quickly give each other a parting hug or do whatever ritualistically brings their time together to an end. As soon as Dad leaves, the child needs to go shut off the alarm clock.

Finally, Mom and the child should have preplanned some high-interest activity to do immediately after Dad leaves.

During periods of stress, a preschool boy's behavior might revert back to earlier habits. He might begin sucking his thumb again, or looking for that old security blanket you'd finally thought he'd given up. He may throw tantrums in frustration, and may become fearful and insecure, suddenly demanding you leave the lights on at night, or running after you and clinging to you whenever you leave him for a while. He may follow you from room to room, watching you with eagle-eyed intensity and panicking if he looks up to suddenly find you gone, and he's likely to want to occupy your lap whenever you sit down. Sleep disturbances are common, and you may find yourself having trouble putting him down to bed in the evening, or he may become restless in the night, waking often, and he may begin bed-wetting. Even if he'd been sleeping well in his own bed up until this point, your son may suddenly start to ask to sleep in your bed with you. Your son may suddenly become your little shadow. What can you do to help your preschool son through this difficult period?

REACTING TO REGRESSION: NOTES FROM DR. HALL

The first thing is not to panic. When your son is going through a difficult time, his behavior is apt to regress. He might revert back to displaying behaviors that you thought he had outgrown, such as sucking his thumb, speaking in "baby talk," or wanting to be held a lot more. His regression may scare you, and you might be so upset by it that you forbid it. You tell him to stop sucking his thumb or push him away when he tries yet again to crawl into your lap. Don't. Your child is doing what he needs to do at this upsetting time to comfort himself. If the circumstance that brought on this regression is a one-time event, like

Dad moving out of the home, your son will make adjustment within a month or two or the regression-like acts will fade away. After all, children are biologically driven to be independent and to mature. All they need is a reasonable, normal, safe environment and they will.

However, bad things do happen to children, such as being sexualized by an unsuspected adult or older child. When that happens, the child is apt to regress, and the regression will not fade. So, as a diligent mom, you will want to monitor your child's actions. If he continues to display regressed behavior for more than six weeks, you might then want to obtain professional help.

Reassurance and comforting is key at this time. Give him lots of hugs and "I love yous" every day. Explain over and over that Daddy's leaving wasn't caused by anything your son did, but that it was because Mom and Dad do best if they don't live together. It's also important to dispel any notions the child might have that Mom and Dad are going to get back together again. A reunion is a common fantasy for children of this age, and while it may seem harmless to go along with their hopes, it actually can prevent them from moving ahead with their new lives. Take care not to inadvertently play into the fantasy by planning to include Dad in family outings or holiday celebrations, at least not for quite a while. While it's wonderful when parents can put aside their differences and be friends even after a divorce, and that's something we should all strive for if it's at all possible, recreating earlier family scenes can be painful for the child. Those only serve to remind the child of what life was like before and heightens their longing to have it back again.

You should assure your child of what the living arrangements are, and remind him of the permanence of those arrangements. Also go over any emergency arrangements you've made for your son's care. If you've agreed with a friend or relative to pick your son up from day care on days you're running behind, go over that plan with your son frequently so he's not shocked or bewildered when you're not there. A child with a single mom often comes to view her as the scope of his world, and may feel that she's the only bridge to security he has, and he may worry what would become of him if anything happened to her. Always project calm and confidence, even if you're faking it. As the saying goes, "fake it until you can make it."

Explain the situation to any other care providers, such as day-care teachers, or babysitters, and go over how you need them to react to various situations so they're not sending conflicting signals to what the child is hearing at home.

Becoming Aware of His Masculine Identity

Studies have shown that boys don't really begin to form a sense of gender identification until about thirty-six months. Suddenly, though, at around that time, your son may become fascinated with all things male. He's likely to suddenly develop a love of combative play, and will begin to distinguish between things he thinks identify a male and things that are for females. He'll become more aware that the media portrays certain activities and toys as being for boys, and others are directed at girls. This is when he's going to begin to build sexual stereotypes, and begin to identify himself along the boy lines. This is also your chance to start to ensure he'll be an open-minded and non-sexist male, who is proud of his own male identity but also respectful of females.

Older preschool boys are definitely much more interested in modeling after adult males. You may find them tagging along behind older boys and male relatives, and you might see your son mirroring postures, gestures, and phrases he's seen older males using. He may even want to dress in similar clothes. He's starting to look to other males for signals on how to behave as a boy, and it's important to give him role models that support your values, and to have other boys around for him to interact and play with. He's too young for formal mentoring, but be sure to make your son aware of positive attributes in the males around him to give him a positive sense of himself as a male. If your son's doctor is very compassionate, you can point out, "Isn't Doctor Brown a very caring man?" If you spot a young man helping an older person get out of a car, you can remind your son, "That's a very nice boy to be so gentle and helpful." Praise your son for all the things you like and admire about him, and celebrate those things that are uniquely male. Be aware of your own history with men, and be careful not to "male-bash" in front of your son. He's just starting to gain a sense of himself as a male, and you want him to take pride in his masculinity.

> "My younger son saw a commercial on TV for a very girly toy, like Barbie, and he said to me, 'You like that, Mommy. You want that toy.' And I told him, 'No, I don't. I never liked Barbie.' He seemed very confused about this. Then my mother explained to my son that my brother had played with Barbie when he was little, and my mother had driven trucks and built houses. Just when my youngest thought he had the whole gender thing all figured out, we totally confused him!"
>
> *Rachel, mother of two*

Talking to Your Preschooler about His Body

It's important to begin talking with your son about his body and being healthy as soon as he begins exploring his body. Bath time is a good time to talk about body parts and give things their proper names, keeping it natural and casual. After all, you teach them, "this is your ear, this is your knee," so they can also learn "this is your penis." Your preschooler probably delights in himself, and while as females (with our own personal history to cope with) we might not be quite as comfortable as he is with his avid exploration and handling of himself, it's important not to teach him shame or embarrassment. Of course, he'll need to learn that some things can't be done out in public, but he should be gently and calmly reminded that some body parts are private. If your son innocently displays his penis in public, don't overreact or make too big a deal out of it (and try not to laugh, either!), since he'll only be intrigued that what he did got such a big reaction and he may be encouraged to do it again! Just keep reminding him that penises are private.

If you son has a sister or other girls he sees unclothed, he's no doubt aware of the differences, though for a while still there may be some confusion over whether or not things might change in the future. Many little girls assume they may someday grow penises, and quite a few little boys wonder about that, too! Now's the time to begin explaining that all girls have vulvas and vaginas, while boys have penises and testicles, and that they'll stay the way they were born, and later on that difference will be important when they want to become mommies and daddies. Explain that a little girl's vulva is private, just like a little boy's penis, and that having a vagina doesn't mean she has less than a boy or is missing something, but that a girl's parts are just as special and important as a boy's, they're just inside, not outside.

Talking about Sexual Predators

This is also a good time to start talking about good touching and bad touching, and to let your son know that he should say "no!" to any people who try to touch him in his private places or asks him to touch theirs, or if someone shows them to him, and that he should immediately tell you if any of these things happen. Again, this type of talk should be handled calmly so as not to make your son fearful or overly concerned. Teaching our sons to beware of sexual predators, both male and female, is something we should begin early and continue with long into their adolescence. Remind your son that no one should ever tell him to keep secrets from you, and that he can always tell you anything that happens and you will always protect and take care of him.

Teach him what to be careful of, and role-play the various tricks and devices predators use to lure children so that your child will recognize when he's being tricked. Many predators will ask the child to come see a puppy or kitten they claim to have in the car, or ask the child's help looking for a puppy that's lost. Explain that no good grown-up would ever ask a child to do that, and that if someone needed help, they'd ask another grown-up, not a child. Others will offer the child a toy, candy, or other treasure if he gets into the car, or may claim they've come to pick up the child because mommy's sick. Explain that you would never send a stranger to get your son, and tell him what your emergency plans are should you ever really be unable to get him personally.

Recent studies have shown that it's not enough to talk about safety with strangers, but that you need to do real world demonstrations and role-playing. In a study designed to determine how effective classroom instruction about safety with strangers could be, youngsters were instructed and then tested in a class about the dangers of talking to a stranger. Afterward, parents took the children to a park, where they sat at a safe distance with an instructor while a second instructor the children hadn't met attempted to lure the child away to search for a lost puppy. Every single child walked away with the stranger. Obviously, talking isn't enough. Take your son out into the real world, into environments where abductions occur, such as playgrounds, the grocery store, or even the front yard of your home, and act out the situation. You might even enlist the help of an adult you know (but your child doesn't) to act the part of the stranger. Repeat these lessons often, in different ways and in different places, so the protective "no!" response becomes automatic.

Again, remind your child over and over that no good grown-up offers anything directly to a child, but would ask the mother first if the child could have something. I often give children small trinkets I win at carnivals or raffles, but I'm careful to always offer it to the parent, both to respect their right to say "no" and to not alarm them as to my intent. I'm pleased with how many parents take that opportunity to talk to their child about how it would be all right for me to do that, but wrong if an adult tried to give him a toy directly without the parent's knowledge.

Be sure to teach your youngster that predators come in all shapes and sizes. They aren't all creepy-looking men lurking in dark alleyways. They can be the grandfatherly type who looks like Santa, a high school kid, a woman, or even someone your child knows. The rules of bad touching apply to everyone.

Finally, you can check out your neighborhood or the one around your school or playground by visiting the Department of Justice National Sex Offender Public Registry Web site at *www .nsopr.gov.*

TEACHING SAFETY WITH STRANGERS

Dr. Karyn Purvis, who specializes in the recovery of abused and traumatized children, suggests moms start talking to their sons about "safe" people starting at a very early age, stressing that "safe" people won't tell you to keep secrets, and they won't touch you without permission. You can also instruct your child as to who is safe to go to for hugs and affection. Teach your child to be communicative and to protect his own body, and to demand others respect themselves. But moms need to realize that almost anyone could pose a potential risk to your child, so every mother needs to be alert, vigilant, and cautious.

As a Mom of a Remarkable Boy, you

- Continue to provide lots of affection, cuddling, and love;
- Keep familiar surroundings and routines if possible;
- Provide day care at home if you can;
- Get the help needed both emotionally and physically;
- Begin to talk with your son about his body so he can develop a healthy body image;
- Make certain he is aware of good and bad touching, and how to be safe with strangers;
- Give constant reassurance that he is not responsible for his father's absence;
- Are positive, calm, and confident; and
- Refuse to enforce sexual stereotypes and gender conformity.

CHAPTER 3

The Middle Years

C hances are, your son's early years were days filled with cuddling and snuggling, where he was your best pal and constant companion. So it might be a little disconcerting as your son goes off to school and begins to pull away and become more and more independent.

Emotional Development

It is normal and healthy for a child to start to show signs of independence starting around the time he enters elementary school. This maturation should be accepted and encouraged. At the same time, remember that your son still needs lots of love, warmth, and affection, and plenty of "I love yous!" Don't make the mistake of thinking that you need to push him away to prevent him from becoming a "mama's boy." In fact, the withdrawal of affection and open displays of love are very damaging to a young boy's emotional health. He may not initiate quite as many hugs as he did as a younger child, and he may begin to feel a bit awkward about you kissing him goodbye in front of other kids, but he should still be receiving plenty of cuddling. Boys in this age group seem to be like a yo-yo on a string, one minute holding tight and climbing on your lap for a hug, the next far away and wiping off the kisses you plant on his cheek! A warm and reassuring bedtime ritual of back rubs and hugs while winding down from the day is a wonderful way to reconnect and give your son the daily dose of affection and cuddling he still craves.

You'll notice that your son will begin to pull away a bit at this age, becoming less open and expressive about his emotions, and he will begin to take time to be by himself to process what's going on inside him before he can talk about it, if he chooses to discuss it at all.

Moms often don't understand this change, and are hurt by it, but it's all part of growing up male instead of female. Boys process emotions differently than girls do, and these may feel foreign and strange to a female. However, it's not a rejection—it's biology! Boys' brains are actually different from those of girls, and this difference in handling emotions is hard-wired. We'll look into this more in Chapter 10.

Developing a Competitive Edge

You might also notice that your son becomes more openly competitive and may engage in playful insults and teasing with other boys. Moms are often shocked and flustered to overhear their sons bragging wildly about their own abilities in sports or games or other activities while making negative comments about their friends' skills. Females would rarely engage in a round of "You suck!," "No, you suck more!" while playing a game with their best friends, but for boys, it's all part of the game and part of routine male interaction. It's normal and harmless and for them, part of the fun. Naturally, that doesn't mean one boy should be allowed to bully another or say truly hurtful things, and you need to be alert to actual cruelty or malice. But for boys, greeting each other with an exchange of "Hey, butt-head," or swapping insults and jostling shoulders while playing on the video game system is nothing to be alarmed about and not grounds for a lecture. As females raising males, we need to understand boys' different ways of interacting.

This period is also the time when your son will become very actively involved in discovering his masculinity. He'll likely become much more interested in older male relatives and your male friends, and you may find him tagging along behind them and picking up their gestures and mannerisms. This is the time you need to become more acutely aware of your son's need for male role models and alert to what he's learning from the older males around him. Involving your son in groups with involved male leaders like Cub Scouts and Boy Scouts, and encouraging him to participate in soccer or Little League, and perhaps exploring the opportunities through Big Brothers of America, will provide him with the male interaction and guidance he'll be needing. If your school has male teachers in your son's grade level, you may want to consider enrolling him in a male-headed classroom. Providing male mentors is discussed more in depth later in this book.

While you should be accepting and encouraging of your son's new interest in the outside world and bonding with male mentors, you should also keep yourself involved in your son's life as he transitions from a life based around home and family and into a life revolving around school, sports, and friends. Volunteer at your son's school. Host activities and participate in field trips, meetings, and dinners. If you're up to the challenge, you could even volunteer to help coach a team! Parental involvement in school is linked to better performance and enjoyment, and supporting sports by coaching, attending, or otherwise boosting your son's teams results in higher self-esteem and feelings of achievement.

Talking to Your Preadolescent about Sex, Drugs, and Peer Pressure

It's never too early to begin to discuss sex and other health issues with your child. The earlier and more openly you're able to talk about these issues, the more comfortable your son will be when he has real questions or issues facing him. It's also important to start early because many parents are surprised to learn that children are much more aware and exposed to issues of sex and drug use while still in elementary school. Moms need to start teaching the facts before the outside world can begin painting the fantasy!

"The Talk"

Even before your son reaches his teen years, the media and his peer group will have been sending messages regarding sexuality, violence, and drug use—quite likely messages that are quite different from what you're trying to teach in your home. In 2005, Nielsen statistics of TV viewership showed that ABC's show *Desperate Housewives* was the most popular broadcast viewed by kids ages nine to twelve! Even when parents think they're being careful about what their kids watch, kids are still being exposed to sexual themes and messages. It was estimated that 6.6 million children under the age of twelve viewed the 2004 Super Bowl halftime show where Justin Timberlake ripped open Janet Jackson's stage costume and exposed her breast.

Some estimates based on average TV viewing by children (calculated to be four hours per day) have stated that children will be exposed to 100,000 acts of violence in the media by the end of their elementary school years. Add to that violence inherent in a great many video games. The media's also sending out strong messages on alcohol. Drinking and drug use is depicted as daring, exotic, and grown-up, something extremely appealing to young males.

You can't completely control the messages your son will be receiving, but you can certainly do a great deal to educate him to make good choices and understand the realities of sex, drug use, and even violence.

Most boys are able to understand a standard "birds and bees" chat by the time they're eight years old, but body differences, pregnancy, and other topics should be a regular part of discussion with your son from the time he's a preschooler so that the ground-work has been laid and the "big talk" is simply a continuation of normal dialogue around your home. You might want to use any of the numerous wonderful books on talking about sex to find the right words and perhaps some basic pictures. Boys should be imbued with a sense of pride in their bodies and in what they are equipped to do, and also a sense of awe and respect.

If you're uncomfortable talking, though, your son will sense this, and that could make him uncomfortable or give him a sense that what you're talking about is shameful or bad. So if you find yourself tense and nervous, admit it and let him know why. Often, we grew up in homes ourselves where no one talked openly about sex, so as moms we don't have the language or skills to do it ourselves. If you're truly uncomfortable with this, call on a trusted adult male relative, such as an uncle or grandfather, to do it. It's a good idea to have a talk first with the "teacher" and be sure you're on the same page about how things should be dis-cussed and what attitudes you want to pass on.

One of the most important messages you can pass along to your young son is the coupling of physical intimacy and true caring and love, and that's a message that's most often lacking in the media depictions your son will be exposed to. Reinforce why intimacy belongs within the context of a committed relationship, and why it makes it special and meaningful.

Talk about the impacts of sex, and about safe sex and preg-nancy prevention. Dispel misconceptions like "girls can't get pregnant the first time," or "girls can't get pregnant during their periods." Kids pick up an amazing amount of wrong, danger-ous, and misinterpreted information about sex from each other or misguided older siblings. The best way to find out what your son knows, or thinks he knows, is to ask.

Explain the facts behind sexually transmitted diseases. It's esti-mated that 93 percent of children will have heard of AIDS by the time they're eight years of age, but for most it's a cloudy and confusing issue, and for some it can cause fear. Can they catch it from sharing a water fountain? What if they get someone else's blood on their skin on the playground? Will their diabetic friend develop AIDS from the needles he uses for insulin? How can a baby be born with HIV? Does that mean anybody can have it?

You should take time to educate your son to the facts in a calm and reassuring manner. He should know that it takes very intimate contact and exchange of bodily fluids with an infected person to become infected with HIV, that he can't get it from using a public restroom or drinking fountain, and that clean needles don't contain any germs and can't make a person sick. He should, however, be cautioned to be extremely careful if he spots a needle lying around on the ground, at the beach, or on top of a trash can, and he should be taught to alert an adult to the presence of needles and not to touch it himself. You can also go a long way to teach compassion and empathy for those living with HIV and AIDS, as well as other serious illnesses.

Alcohol and Drugs

Along with an earlier introduction to sexual issues, alcohol use by school-age children is also on the rise, and reports by the U.S. Surgeon General and the 2005 National Survey on Drug Use and Health indicate many children begin drinking as early as eight or nine years of age and even more report drinking regularly by the time they've reached age twelve. What can you do to prevent your son from becoming an underage drinker? Talking with your son is your greatest weapon. Establish the rules of your house, and that those rules include no underage drinking. Explain the many adverse impacts of drinking, on health, learning, and families. Talk about your own experiences when you've seen alcohol hurt people and ruin lives. Point out articles in the news where youngsters have been hurt and even died from alcohol, and how that could have been avoided. Practice with your son how to avoid situations where alcohol may be offered, and how to react if it is. Furthermore, alert other parents if you know or suspect that any drinking is going on. Underage drinking is more likely to be avoided if adults don't allow alcohol into the hands of underage kids. If you have alcohol in your home, keep it locked where children cannot gain access to it. Most kids begin drinking by sneaking beer, wine, or liquor out of the family fridge or cabinet.

Finally, be aware of the example you're setting with your own alcohol use in front of your son. If you reach for a drink the moment you come home from work, or during a stressful period, your son will be learning that that's the natural way to relax or cope with problems.

Use the moments when alcohol appears in a TV show or advertisement to talk about it. What's the real message of the advertising? Are they trying to say you'll be cool if you drink this, or girls will find you attractive? Discuss how the companies use these messages to encourage people to drink, and why a smart person can outsmart the messages. Instead, make it cool to say "no."

It's also important to lay the groundwork early for drug prevention. Younger kids can be introduced to drugs by older siblings, older friends, even, shockingly, by adults in the community, so don't assume a child is too young to come into contact with drugs. Talk to your child about the dangers of drug use. Younger kids and teens are especially susceptible to rapid addiction, so your child must understand that experimentation can be life altering, and quite possibly, lethal.

Bring up the "non-drug" methods kids use to get high. "Huffing," or inhaling the fumes or vapors from aerosols, can lead to intoxication, but it can also kill almost immediately. If you find your child in possession of any substance that seems suspicious, out-of-place, or difficult to explain, confiscate it. You're always better off safe than sorry.

And even if a child is aware that illicit drugs are dangerous, he may be tempted to try a prescription medication he finds in the medicine cabinet. Kids will share drugs they're given for pain, for attention deficit disorder (ADD), for depression, or even anti-psychotics, not realizing the extreme danger in giving a medication to someone it hasn't been prescribed for. You need to talk openly with your son about the dangers of *all* drugs, not just ones sold on the street. If your child must take a medication, stress to him that he must never share it with anyone. Keep track of how many doses should be in the bottle, and if any seem to be missing. If possible, always have your child take his doses in front of you, and under no circumstances should he be allowed to carry his meds with him outside the house.

If you take prescription medications, talk to your son about what they're for, and why no one else should try taking them without a doctor's orders. Then keep the meds under lock and key. Even if your child is completely trustworthy, other people visiting your home may not be. I've listed several very useful drug prevention Web sites in the appendix of this book, and they offer wonderful advice on creating an anti-drug message.

Media Messages: Violence and Your Son

Your son isn't just exposed to tempting images of alcohol and drug use in the media; he's also being inundated with messages about violence in everything from his music, to TV, to the video games aimed at young males. You must work to counteract the violence your son may be exposed to, and to make him aware of the messages and mindset the media may be promoting. Carefully monitor the video games he plays for violent content and ban the ones that are inappropriate to children. Any game that is rated MA should never be in the hands of children. Many of these games use extremely realistic, graphic violence, and often violence against women, as their big lure. Games like Grand Theft Auto depict the player having sex with prostitutes, and then even award extra points for killing the prostitute after the encounter! Be aware of the dreadful messages these games are sending out. Especially when boys become deeply involved with games, often playing them hours and hours at a time, it's easy for them to absorb what's depicted in them. They lose themselves in the game and "become" their player or character. There are video game magazines and guides that spell out the content of the games, and you should never buy or allow your son to be given a game unless you're aware of the content. Make it clear to him that you do not want him to play these games at other kids' houses, either, and explain to him why the games are wrong and dangerous. Provide him with healthier alternatives. If he's intent on playing video games, he'll likely enjoy the new interactive games, like those for the Nintendo Wii system, that allow the player to jump, jog, and pretend to ski, bat, and participate in other activities that will get him off the floor and moving around!

You can also limit the types of movies and TV shows your son watches. Since 1999, all TVs have come equipped with a V-chip that allows parents to control what shows can be viewed based on ratings. TV shows rating G, Y, and Y7 are safe for viewing by young children, with the G- and Y-rated shows containing no violence or sexual depictions, and the Y7 shows limited to only mild, comedic violence (such as cartoon characters bopping each other), or fantasy violence like dragons. PG shows are best watched with adult supervision but are quite mild and acceptable.

As a mother, you can be the single most important influence in your growing son's life. Constant open, honest communication, coupled with a strong, positive role model (you!) can equip your child with the tools he'll need to make sound decisions, now and later on in life. But far beyond influencing his attitudes toward harmful elements, you also have a golden opportunity to use your communication and personal time together with your preadolescent son to affirmatively establish opportunities for learning, and for developing lifelong healthy habits.

Your role isn't limited to being gatekeeper, blocking out and countering the dangerous and negative elements your son will encounter. You're also the key to broadening horizons and creating strong, positive attitudes. Your school-age son has a tremendous capacity for learning and an immense curiosity about the world around him. Exposing him during this period to new ideas, creative ways of problem solving, and interesting career options will open up new worlds for him, and will be immense fun for you, too! And starting to explore new worlds can start right in your own home!

Creating a Learning-Friendly Home

Learning opportunities abound. Take time to explain things to your son as you go through your day. Even a young child can absorb an amazing amount of knowledge though casual observation and everyday conversation. As you work in your garden or with houseplants, explain why you're fertilizing the soil or pruning a plant. Explain how a wheelbarrow allows you to lift and push more than you could lift using your arms alone. As you're cooking, talk about how heating the water causes the molecules to move faster, and bump into each other, and eventually turn into water vapor (steam). You can even spontaneously do demonstrations and experiments. If heat makes molecules bump against each other and take up more room, what happens when the air in a balloon gets hotter or colder? Blow air into a balloon and tie it outside to observe the change. Even getting stuck in traffic is an opportunity to talk about traffic patterns and population or driving techniques, or gas consumption. Never let an opportunity pass you by! Explain why you're doing something, how it works, and what happens. Once you get into the habit of teaching as a part of everyday life, you'll find new and creative ways to introduce your son to a vast array of subjects.

You should also include learning field trips as a part of your normal family life. Many museums, zoos, planetariums, and aquariums offer family memberships that allow unlimited visits throughout the year and special discounts or free participation in special events, particularly those oriented toward children, and many also allow members to bring along a guest for free (so you can have a friend of your son tag along for free). Many also offer free admittance to other partner facilities. Some zoo memberships allow admittance to zoos and aquariums across the country, so when you're traveling, there's no additional charge to spend the day at a new and exciting place with whole new learning possibilities. You could can visit a new and different zoo every month! National and state parks are a goldmine for learning about geology, natural history, wildlife, and America's past, and are always a bargain for all they offer.

I toured the nation's battlefields with my own sons, who developed a reverence and respect for the sacrifices it took to build our country. Moments like touching cannonballs still lodged in the walls of homes in Yorktown, Virginia, talking about how frightening the siege on the town must have been, and having the boys recreate Pickett's Charge across the vast and silent field at Gettysburg helped us to talk about war. It also allowed them to determine for themselves whether the war was necessary, and why. The kids took so much more away from these experiences than any textbook or novel could have taught them. We must remember, as mothers of sons, that each of our boys will have to register for the selective service, and many will opt to join the military, and it's our responsibility to educate them as to the full meaning of that service so that their decisions come from a place of knowledge and understanding. Learning is so much more than just science, or math. Offer your son an education in life, in values, and in choices.

Apart from museums, zoos, nature centers, and other more expected field trip adventures, check out the possibilities with local businesses. Our local recycling plant opens to families several times a year, offering tours that show how plastic, metal, paper, and glass are gathered and turned into new products and the environmental benefits of recycling. Kids get to wear hard hats and goggles, and boys seem to delight in "talking trash" and watching the big machines do their jobs.

> "I noticed in the paper that there was something called a Smart Living Center nearby offering an open house during the school vacation. I had no idea what it was, but I packed the kids into the car and off we went! And I was really amazed once we got there. There were hands-on experiments for the kids and demonstrations of energy efficient products and even free cookies and juice. The boys spent the entire morning there and I had to drag them out when it was time to leave. If I hadn't been feeling adventurous, we would have missed a great chance to learn something new."
>
> —*Rachel, mother of two boys*

Check with local facilities to find out when their community and educational programs are offered.

Boy-Friendly Field Trips

Recycling plants: As mentioned above, these are fun, educational, and encourage environmental awareness.

Power plants: These teach about the generation and conservation of electricity and the demands of a growing population on power, and how kids can save electricity in their homes and schools.

Manufacturing facilities: Boys have a natural love of learning how things are built and taken apart. Whether the plant makes cars, motorcycles, trucks, glassware, boxes, or candy, look into a tour, whether as a family or through your son's school. Mister Rogers' Neighborhood, the children's show on PBS, knew the intrinsic fascination of showing how familiar things are made and frequently highlighted a visit to a crayon factory or toy manufacturing shop. Continue to foster this curiosity by taking your son behind the scenes. These are places where kids jump at the chance to ask questions.

Farms and orchards: Foster your son's love of living things and a respect for the land and the environment by visiting organic and naturally run farms and orchards. Lots of smaller farms enjoy talking about their operations with visitors, teaching about the growing cycle, water use, and natural alternatives to pesticides for insect control. A small farm here in Connecticut offers summer camps where kids do the farm chores, feed and care for rescue animals, and learn about real life on a farm. The kids are exhausted and smelling of manure by the end of the day, but they love it!

The Kitchen as a Learning Laboratory

Working with your son in the kitchen can be a major learning boom for your school-age (and even preschool!) son. Cooking involves working with weights and measures, time and temperatures, even chemical reactions, all through the hands-on method boys thrive on! It teaches creativity while at the same time illustrating the need for careful attention to details and instructions. It's also a great opportunity to interact and socialize with your child since it provides the helpful activity that facilitates communicating with boys. Finally, studies have shown that a child who eats well does better in school, has fewer behavior problems, maintains a healthier weight, and has fewer dietary-linked health issues like diabetes.

Working with measuring spoons and cups teaches fractions and proportions. It's a snap to illustrate using dry ingredients how, for example, three one-third cup measures equal the same amount as one full cup, and how five one-quarter cup measures is the same as one full cup and one quarter cup. It's also a great time to introduce the metric system. Many glass measuring cups are marked off in both metric and English measurements, so your son can begin to understand equivalencies and how to convert.

Cooking is also a great time to start to talk about proper nutrition and healthy eating. Teach your son to critically evaluate the nutritional labels on packaged foods, and what to look for. Discuss how much sodium, sugar, or fat is healthy and how to make the healthiest choices. Boys love to be given the task of reading the labels and making suggestions as to what's good and what's not. Even my six-year-old grandson is able to pull boxes off the shelf in the grocery store and let us know if the salt or sugar content is too high, and he's a demon when it comes to zeroing in on labels that advertise 100 percent organic.

Cooking is also an essential life skill for any young person to master. A boy who knows how to cook will be less dependent on fast food and packaged convenience foods. And let's not forget, girls love a boy who can cook for them! It shows sensitivity, nurturing, and caring, as well as a worldly maturity and self-reliance.

Boys can be taught to weigh, measure, and mix dry ingredients by the age of five, and are especially excited when they get to help with making special holiday foods and family favorites. Naturally, young children need to be kept away from hot surfaces and cooking pots, and any preteen needs careful supervision in the kitchen at all times, but even the youngest child can be taught to begin enjoying preparing food. Toddlers can be allowed to help wash veggies in the sink with a vegetable brush while standing on a stool, and can help mix dry ingredients with a large spoon. Feeling useful and helpful fosters pride of accomplishment and personal satisfaction in your son and having responsibilities around the house should be a necessary part of growing up.

The new silicon bakeware on the market is especially kid-friendly since it's unbreakable and reduces the risk of burns or other injury, and the kids love popping things out of them. They're also easy to clean up, which is also bound to gain the appreciation of any boy assigned to do the dishes.

There are lots of recipes that you can allow your son to experiment with to encourage his love of cooking and bolster his natural creativity. Once he's got the hang of the basics, introduce him to cooking shows and books by male chefs like Bobby Flay, Emeril, and Mario Battali.

Boy-Friendly Dishes:

Pizza: What boy doesn't love pizza? You can start out with pre-baked pizza crusts (they even come in healthy whole wheat now) and allow him to add sauces, shredded cheeses, and a variety of toppings. Mini-pizzas can be made using split English muffins or bagels, or you can use a loaf of Italian or French bread sliced open. Encourage him to mix it up, trying different cheeses, making "white pies" and unusual and exotic toppings. As an insurance policy, try making the pie in quarters with different toppings on each quarter, just in case that foray into okra and sardines wasn't as successful as your son was hoping. In time, you can start experimenting with raw pizza dough and allowing your son to roll or hand-spread the dough into a crust and trying out thin crust, thick crust, and even deep dish styles. Your son will be the hit of the neighborhood with his homemade special pizzas!

Chef Salad: With your son as 'chef,' this dish can be anything he wants. Any combination of vegetables, fruits, nuts, meats, cheeses, and dressings can be tossed together in unique and endless variety. Experiment with baby lettuces and baby spinach (dark green leafy ones have the most nutrition!), crumble and thin slice cheeses, add fish like tuna or salmon if you want, add some chopped nuts and slices of fresh apple, orange sections, or kiwi slices, nearly anything you can think of!

Trail Mix: A handy favorite for after-school snacking or tossing in a lunch bag. Have your son take a large size zipper close plastic bag and pour in nuts, seeds, dried fruit like dried banana slices, cherries, raisins, or pineapple pieces, some chocolate chips or peanut butter chips, and perhaps even some dried seasoned veggies like dried peas.

Fun Fruit Parfaits: Your son can mix fresh or partly thawed frozen berries with whipped cream or fat-free non-dairy topping, and add sliced almonds or walnuts on top for extra nutrition.

As a Mom of a Remarkable Boy, you

- Understand your son's natural male differences in emotional expression;
- Still provide lots of love, hugs, and affection;
- Help your son seek out positive male mentors;
- Talk openly about sex, drugs, and violence;
- Counter negative media depictions and discuss the inappropriate messages boys are receiving; and
- Find new and interesting ways to explore the world around him.

CHAPTER 4

The Teen Years

Your son is changing in so many ways right before your eyes at this stage. There may be moments when you wonder if he's even the same child! One moment he may be sweet and considerate, still asking for back rubs and chatting with you ceaselessly, and the next he may be a snarling stranger, slamming doors and declaring "No one understands me!" And chances are, your teen son probably doesn't even understand himself all of the time.

Physiological Changes

Your teen son's body is developing and maturing extremely rapidly at this time, and some of those changes started several years earlier without any outward sign. Sometime around the age of ten in boys, the hypothalamus signals changes in the body's hormones, stimulating the pituitary gland. The pituitary then releases its own hormones, stimulating the gonads and the adrenal glands, and those begin producing and releasing testosterone and androgens that cause the sex organs to grow and mature. The first outward sign of puberty in boys usually occurs around the age of thirteen, and the process might continue all the way to the age of twenty. However, some boys don't really begin puberty until the age of sixteen, and sons have to be assured that there's a normal range of ages for different visible changes to occur, so though he might be ahead or behind his friends or the kids in the locker room, he's still normal. If he's a late bloomer, let him know he'll eventually catch up and there's nothing wrong with him. Similarly, if he matures more rapidly than his friends and is embarrassed by this, assure him that there is nothing abnormal about this, and that others will catch up.

As the flood of hormones begins, the testicles will begin to grow larger, and will actually continue to gain size for about six years. Shortly after the testes begin their growth, the penis and scrotum follow suit, and the penis typically continues to grow until the age of about eighteen. Boys will begin to experience erections and orgasms very frequently, and ejaculations become possible for the first time. Pubic hairs begin to appear around the same time as the sex organs begin to grow larger, and much later, hair will become thicker on the thighs and the abdomen extending upward to the navel. Boys will also begin to develop body hair and facial hair, though the amount of body hair varies widely between men, often depending on ethnicity, and appears quite different from one boy to the next.

Even before the appearance of facial hair, and around the time you see your son shooting up through one size of clothes after another, you'll notice your son's voice getting deeper. Boys' voices don't necessarily "break," but they may sometimes have difficulty controlling their changing, deepening voices. This phase is often very short-lived and ends as the boy learns to "train" and modulate his new, deeper voice a bit better.

In many pubescent boys, you'll also notice that a small "breast bud" or even fairly significant breast growth may develop temporarily, and this condition is sometimes exaggerated by a bit of extra body fat. It typically diminishes on its own as puberty wanes, and isn't cause for alarm, and isn't a sign that a boy has too many female hormones or is abnormal! However, if it bothers your son a great deal, there is a surgical remedy for it, and you should consult your son's doctor to discuss your options.

Boys also gain a great deal of muscle mass and bone mass, and you'll especially notice your son's jaw growing larger and his shoulders growing broader. Your son might also temporarily seem to be all arms and legs, and might become a bit more ungainly as he has to learn to maneuver within his new dimensions. Consider what it must feel like to suddenly lose track of how far your reach is, or how long your feet are! In some boys, growth spurts can affect sports performance from time to time, but boys should be assured that they shouldn't take it too hard, and they'll likely outgrow any slump simply through experience.

The Amazing Changing Teenage Brain!

Just as the rest of a teen's body is changing rapidly and dramatically, so is the teen brain. In fact, the adolescent brain is undergoing a process akin to rewiring itself. It's a period of confusion, mixed signals, and exaggerated and difficult-to-understand emotional reactions. Have you ever found yourself exclaiming to your teen, "What on earth were you thinking?" As you'll see here, your teen son will likely be as stumped as you!

In an adult brain, the prefrontal area is involved with such processes as judgment, planning, and insight. This is the part of the brain that allows you to clearly think through something you're going to do and examine and consider the consequences before making a decision whether to do it or not. The frontal lobes are involved in inhibiting behaviors and moral decisions about actions. This portion of the brain also interacts with the emotional part of the brain, so in processing emotions, adults are tapping into reason and judgment.

However, in a teen brain, this important prefrontal region isn't engaged nearly as much as it is in adults when making decisions. Instead, brain researchers have discovered, what's firing away in the teen brain is the much more emotional, gut response region called the amygdala. This region handles the well-known fight-

or-flight reactions like fear and anger. Teen brains are accessing the amygdala because the frontal lobe region of the brain is developing rapidly during this time of life, producing new gray matter that's not entirely mature and that has inefficient connections within it. The brain is functionally rewiring itself, taking the frontal lobe area temporarily off-line to a large degree because of its inefficient connections and communication.

Because the frontal lobes aren't engaged as fully in adolescents, kids may have problems controlling their emotions or responding appropriately to situations and stimuli, as well as a host of other difficulties. Experiments performed by Deborah Yurgelun-Todd and her colleagues at the McLean Hospital Brain Imaging Center in Boston compared brain activity in adults and in teens when presented with a series of pictures. The subjects were asked to determine what emotion the person in the picture was demonstrating. Teen brains accessed the gut response amygdala during the task, as opposed to the adults, who were using the higher function frontal lobes. The surprising result was that the teen subjects misread the emotions in the pictures they were viewing. The implications for real-life situations for teens are obvious. If teens are misreading facial cues and other communication cues, how can they respond appropriately or correctly? Teens are likely to misunderstand and fly off the hook or feel an exaggerated reaction, even in normal conversation with an adult, such as their mothers. Teens are also likely to have more interpersonal relationship problems with friends, teachers, and others because of their misjudgments.

The stronger response from the amygdala and the relative weak engagement of the frontal lobes also suggests teens will have poor impulse control and judgment, acting impulsively and irrationally, engaging in risky or dangerous behavior without any thought or recognition of the dangers they're exposing themselves to. While kids are able to learn to use good judgment and to make wise decisions, it's unwise for parents to assume that just because a teen is looking more mature and adult-like, he's equipped with an adult's reasoning. At this phase of their lives, teens are simply not wired to always make sound judgment calls. Moms need to exercise caution in allowing too much decision-making freedom in their teen sons and understand and assume that even the most intelligent and responsible teen boy is capable (or even likely) to make some incredibly misguided decisions.

Another fascinating finding of brain researchers is that boys respond more from the "gut level" region of the brain than girls do. Girls use more of the "executive decision-making" area of the brain, even in adolescence. Again, these differences lead to more impulsive, reckless, behavior in males, an issue mothers need to be aware of. Even if you've raised a daughter through the dangerous teen years, don't make assumptions regarding your son's reasoning abilities based on his sister's past history.

Teens will also often have issues with organization, memory, and prioritizing, something that can negatively affect their academic performance. Moms can help by setting up new organizational assistance and routines. For a while, you may have to provide an external system to keep your son on track, since the internal one isn't as reliable! Charts, schedules, and tickler files can all be employed to keep your son from falling behind or forgetting about important events. Examine study skills to see if your child might benefit from new techniques to assist his memory and recall. You should also have regular discussions with your child and his teachers about his school performance and any problems that might appear. Simply because a boy is now in high school doesn't mean he needs less parental involvement at school. Much more on education is covered in Chapter 11.

Teen boys are likely confused, frightened, or even concerned about their sanity at times during their adolescence. They'll likely be frustrated with themselves, bewildered by their own behavior, and feeling out of control, a very scary place to be for kids. It's important to speak to your teen about the changes he's going through, and assure him they are natural and temporary. However, be aware that this is the stage in life that certain very real psychological disorders do first appear.

■ For more information on the changes that occur in the adolescent brain, check out the National Institute of Mental Health's article "Teenage Brain: A Work in Progress" at *www.nimh.nih.gov/Publicat/teenbrain.cfm.*

If you or your son feel that there's a deeper issue, or if you're concerned for your son's safety or his behavior has become extreme, contact your son's physician or your community's mental health services department to consult with a professional.

Emotional Needs of Teens

At this stage of your son's life, his focus is changing dramatically. The center of his life has shifted from home and family to his peer group and the larger community. Your son will want more independence, and may seem to be pulling away at times as he develops his more adult persona. You might even begin to think he doesn't need you anymore! But you couldn't be more wrong.

Keeping the Communication Flowing

Even though your child is beginning to look and act more and more like an adult, he still desperately needs your love, nurturing, and support. Even if he doesn't always answer you back, you should still shower him with "I love yous" and hugs. He still needs to hear how proud you are of him, and that you care deeply about the things that are important to him. Though it may seem like all he cares about are his friends and his life away from home, a large degree of his self-esteem and inner strength still comes from you. All too often, I've heard a teenage boy say dejectedly,

"Oh, my parents don't care," when I knew very well they cared very deeply but were no longer sure how to express it.

Whether you're an elegant wordsmith able to express your innermost feelings to your son with grace and depth, or you're cheering your lungs out at his ballgame, or you just break down and blubber at your son's award ceremony or when he gives you an unexpected hug or compliment, you're expressing how you feel, and that's all that matters. Some moms I know write notes that their sons can read when they're alone, and though they may never even comment on it, the boys carry those words with them for the rest of their lives. If you can't talk, or feel like you're never in the same room together long enough anymore, then write. It doesn't matter how you communicate, as long as you do.

Wanting Independence, Needing Limits

Your teen is probably eager to expand his horizons and have many of his former childhood limits lifted. But you still need to proceed with caution. While teens need to experiment with decision making, it shouldn't be at the risk of life and limb.

Teens still need limits and structure, rules and expectations. This isn't the time to throw your hands up and say, "whatever you want is fine with me." As already discussed previously, teens aren't always capable of making rational decisions. Instead, it's best to keep a hand on the parental rudder, sitting by your son's side as you let him make smaller decisions independently, but still insisting on discussion and input (and at times, parental veto) regarding all larger decisions. Small decisions include things like joining clubs, what clothes to buy, or whether to do homework right after school or after dinner. Larger decisions that should require discussion include taking advanced placement or college-level courses, dropping a class, taking a job after school, going on an overnight trip, or house rules such as curfew. Parental veto power needs to be invoked in such decisions as dropping out of high school, participating in a highly dangerous activity, and drinking and drug use. Even if teens look more like adults than children, they haven't developed the insight and bank of knowledge necessary to make larger decisions independently, and they still must recognize and respect your parental authority. Regardless of how they may protest certain of your decisions, you're still communicating that you care, and that is ultimately what your son will remember.

Reaching Outside for Role Models

Even in families with a dad at home, teen boys often begin to focus more on other adult males, seeking out other role models who share interests, or who project qualities your son hopes to emulate. Favorite teachers, coaches, fathers of friends, and formal mentors will begin to take a more vital role in your son's life. Encourage your son's relationships with responsible older male mentors, but still exercise caution and find out as much as you can about the person your son is spending time with. Adults can exert even more pressure on a teen than his peers can, and adults are more skilled at manipulation, so an ill-intentioned or misguided adult can be extremely destructive. Again, keep your hand on the rudder. Talk to your son about other adults in his life, why he enjoys their company, what it is about them he finds interesting or appealing. If your son is excited because a mentor is happy to teach him about cars, or computers, or is just willing to talk about what's going on in his life, that can be reassuring, but be on the lookout for such signs as "he's not like other adults, he's more like a kid" or other indications the adult male might not be mature and responsible or may encourage unhealthy behavior. I encountered too many kid-like adults who thought it was fun to sit around drinking with teens, or who were pathologically immature and encouraged risk-taking behaviors in kids. Even if your son is nearly old enough to go away to college and be on his own, you still need to be extremely aware of who is in his life and what effects others may have on him.

Talking to Your Teen about Sex

At this phase of your son's life, he should already be well versed in the biology of sex and procreation, and aware of both birth control and disease prevention. He should also be aware that celibacy is an acceptable and emotionally responsible lifestyle for any teen, no matter how teen comedies and nighttime TV dramas present it. Sex should not be treated lightly or gratuitously, since it has vast and far-reaching implications and consequences. Unsafe or unhealthy sexual activity can destroy lives with illness, unplanned pregnancy, and emotional pain.

The various methods of preventing pregnancy, both those used by boys and those used by girls, should be discussed and explained in detail, and as most health professionals now advocate, it should be stressed that two forms of birth control are really necessary to completely guard against unexpected pregnancy. Though many forms of birth control boast a nearly perfect statistic for effectiveness, in practice, particularly with inexperienced younger people, the reality is much lower rates of protection simply because the product isn't used or placed properly, or because other circumstances can negatively impact the integrity of the birth control product. There are many drugs and over-the-counter medications and herbal remedies that can adversely affect the effectiveness of birth control pills, for example. Also, condoms can break down and weaken when used with baby oil or petroleum jelly.

Boys need to be given all the information necessary to protect themselves and any sex partner, even if their mothers are thinking or hoping they won't need to put it to use! Educating your teen about sex and discussing birth control is not going to seem like advocating teen sex or endorsing it. In fact, by keeping open and honest dialogue going with your child about sex, you'll help him make more informed and more mature decisions regarding sexual activity. Studies have shown that kids who feel they can talk openly about sex with their parents are less likely to get involved in high-risk sexual behavior. If you feel awkward or uncomfortable talking, be honest about that to your son! It's okay to say, "Sex wasn't mentioned in my house when I was growing up," or, "I was made to feel really embarrassed about sex and I don't want the same thing to happen to you." Finally, it's always fine to have a trusted adult speak with your son if he has a close relationship with someone like an uncle, grandfather, or older cousin or sibling. The key is to make sure your son has *someone* he can turn to for information, advice, and reality checks. Just be sure that the other adult expresses the same values and standards that you want to impart to your child.

Never lose sight in your discussions of the caring, loving aspect of sex. With sex becoming more and more impersonal in the media, it's more and more important to make your son aware of the ultimate treasure, a fully developed relationship involving mutual respect, honesty, devotion, trust, and support.

The Hook-Up

One of the most troubling trends in recent years is the frightening common practice of "hooking-up." Hooking-up involves a non-dating pair of teens getting together solely for the purpose of engaging in sexual activity with no deeper intentions of a romantic relationship or emotional commitment. This practice is going on in large cities and small towns, and often begins as early as early adolescence. Middle school principals have reported coming across young girls performing oral sex on boys in the corridors during the change of classes, and journalists cover stories about groups of high school students getting together after school for casual group sex at an unattended home. Once the territory of single adults, typically in a large city, hooking up has infiltrated down into the teen population, with devastating impacts on both boys and girls.

Consider the long-term implications to the moral and emotional development of boys at this critical point in their lives. Teen boys are fueled by an immense sex drive. They think about it, dream about it, plot and plan, and scheme about how to get it. And though they may be otherwise sensitive and caring people, they are usually still having problems relating to girls, expressing themselves emotionally, and learning how to handle long-term meaningful relationships with females. The lure of the hook-up, with its easy and immediate access to sex without the "fuss and bother" of an actual relationship, can quickly replace the normal course of wooing and winning a girlfriend and building a romantic relationship with its many lessons, pitfalls, perils, and pleasures. How can a teenage boy learn how to be a responsible, reliable, and trustworthy partner later on in life without the early lessons to be learned in his early romantic relationships?

What can be done to discourage kids from this destructive practice? First of all, communication is key. Most hook-ups occur right after school at a house where no adult is present, or at parties where the adults aren't an active and visible presence. Know where your child is, and know who else will be with him. If he's planning to go to a party, check in with the parents and make sure they'll not only be home, but that they'll be on the scene. Communicate with other parents. If you find out a party's going on at a home where no parents are present, inform the other adults. Moms can create an active and effective network to keep kids safe and out of trouble. Get to know your son's friends' parents. Gather home phone numbers, work numbers, and create your own grapevine. Find out who will be out of town when, and watch out for each other's kids. You're not being nosey or intrusive—you're being a parent and you're being responsible. You're letting your child know you care. Boys want limits, they want structure and discipline, and they long to know they're loved. Set down limits, and enforce them.

Communicate with your son, as well, about the harm that hooking-up can do. *Unhooked* by Laura Sessions Stepp is an excellent place to start to learn about the emotional impact hooking-up has on girls, the loss of sense of self-worth and identity, and the deeper issues of depression and drug and alcohol abuse. Most researchers have found alcohol to play a role in hook-ups for young women, not because alcohol heightened their desire or made them less inhibited, but to numb them from the experience and the shame and humiliation. Though the practice seems to have had its origin with women trying to claim the same sexual freedoms as men, it's females who suffer the consequences and are emotionally damaged the most. Teach your son to honor and respect females, and to understand the pain and hurt and loss of self-esteem that demeaning sexual practices inflicts on girls.

If Your Son Is Gay

As will be discussed in more detail in Chapter 6, a growing body of scientific research has supported the understanding that sexual orientation is not a matter of choice but something a person is born with, or predetermined. Brain science studies have shown, time and again, that there are actual physical differences in the brains of homosexual males compared to heterosexual males. And as something that's hard-wired into a child even before birth, sexual orientation isn't something someone is going to outgrow or be conditioned out of. It's as natural a part of that person as is eye color or right- or left-handedness. And as such, sexual orientation needs to be something that's accepted and supported, and never treated with scorn, rejection, or derision. From early on in your son's life, he should be exposed to an accepting attitude toward different sexual orientations, both so that he can lead a more open-minded and enlightened life later on, and also so that he will feel more comfortable with himself and with his feelings should he realize that he is homosexual.

For many moms, particularly single moms, a son's announcement that he's gay is often met with an easy acceptance. Moms often confide they already knew or suspected as much and were simply waiting for their son to decide the time was right to come out. And though many parents may worry about how the rest of the world is going to receive the information, or how their son's sexual orientation may impact certain aspects of his life, they never for one moment worry that their child being gay is a problem or a negative.

If you do suspect your son is gay, or may be experiencing confusion over his sexual orientation or struggling with it, it's important to let him know you want him to feel he can come to you and talk about those feelings and that you'll be accepting and non-judgmental, and that you'll love him every bit as much no matter what.

■ Contact Parents, Families and Friends of Lesbians and Gays (PFLAG) at *www.pflag.org* for more information, education and support.

Educate yourself on the difficulties a homosexual boy may experience emotionally, and be proactive in getting him help if he needs it. Depression and suicide is more common among gay teens because of problems with understanding and accepting their own sexual orientation, and because of the rejection, pressure, prejudice, and even violence some teens experience. Affirmatively protect your son's civil rights. Gay students and citizens are protected from harassment and must be provided with a safe school environment.

Talking to Your Teen about Drug and Alcohol Use

Peer pressure on teens to use alcohol and drugs can be immense. And though national studies have indicated that most kids try alcohol for the first time at age eleven, it usually isn't until the teen years that kids are exposed to drinking and drug use on a large scale, with easy access, sometimes even with the cooperation of adults (even parents) who feel supplying teens with alcohol or drugs is cool or a way to cope with the "inevitable" by having the kids drinking at home under supervision. We've all seen news stories about high school coaches providing alcohol for teen parties, and parents being arrested and held liable for teens who drank in their homes and then tried to drive home, sometimes with tragic consequences. But teen drinking and drug use doesn't have to be inevitable, nor does it have to be accepted, condoned, or ignored by adults.

■ Studies have shown that when kids have good communication with their parents, they're more able to resist peer pressure and make better decisions regarding drinking and drugs. An excellent place to begin to learn about how to talk about this subject with your teen is the Web site Parents, The Anti-Drug at *www.theantidrug.com*. This Web site gives lists of symptoms of drug and alcohol use, suggestions on how to combat teen use, and even a list of common drug terms and slang that parents should be aware of.

During the teen years, it's especially important to avoid drugs and alcohol. The developing brain is particularly vulnerable to these substances, and they can interfere with the building and strengthening of synapses. Teens become addicted much faster and more readily, and teens requiring rehabilitation is becoming all too common. A teen who becomes addicted loses out on so much of his life and becomes vulnerable to relapse for a lifetime. Stress the extreme dangers of drug use at this time of his life with your son.

Keep communication flowing by engaging your son in dialogue rather than in one-way monologues. Ask questions about how your son views drinking, and how his friends see it. Ask why kids try drinking and how your son's peer group or school society view kids who abstain. Discuss how drinking is portrayed in the media, and ask your son how he thinks that influences decisions to drink. Talk openly if there's a history of alcoholism or drug addiction in the family, and how that impacted everyone. As the child of two high-functioning alcoholics, I shared stories with my kids of how that really destroyed our family life when I was young, and emphasized to my kids the higher risk of alcoholism that they are at risk of due to genetics.

Teens often claim that they drink because "there's nothing else to do!" And while that's a pretty lame excuse by any measure, there's plenty of evidence to show that kids who are involved in activities and have a wide range of interests are less likely to become involved with drugs and alcohol. The exception to this rule is certain team sports, where drinking has sometimes become part of the culture. However, parents can largely control and eliminate this behavior by refusing to condone the practice, and by refusing to provide teens with alcohol and aggressively sanctioning, even legally and criminally, those adults who do.

It's particularly important for teen males to have outlets that challenge them and involve them in self-sacrifice for a larger, common good. Volunteer work through church groups, school groups, and civic organizations allow lots of opportunities for boys to feel adult, and to interact with positive role models in adult mentors in appropriate ways and give them the "something better to do" that teens crave. It also builds self-esteem and self-reliance, both of which can boost a kid's resistance to peer pressure. Spending time working at a shelter gives a teen a new respect and appreciation for what he has at home as well as develops his empathy for other people and his sense of larger community. When my son was in culinary school, part of his training required working at a soup kitchen as his community service requirement. He came home at the end of each of those days tired, somber, and humbled. Interacting up close and personal, he came to see that the homeless and poverty-stricken in a new light. He learned their stories and gained a greater understanding. Volunteering at a hospital, becoming a fire cadet, riding with the ambulance corps, even working with younger students as a mentor can all provide a teen boy with the challenge to reach beyond himself and be something greater through giving of himself that will build an inner sense of self that can combat the lure of drugs.

■ For more information on the prevention, detection, and treatment of drug and alcohol issues, check out The National Youth Anti-Drug Media Campaign at *www .mediacampaign.org*. This Web site offers guidelines for parents on talking with their kids about drugs, the latest information on the impact of drug use, and a wealth of other resources. For very specific indicators of the use of individual drugs, such as cocaine, ecstasy, or oxycontin, consult the National Youth Anti-Drug Web site at *www .theantidrug.com.*

As discussed in other chapters, it's also important for moms of teens to establish a strong information network with other mothers and fathers of their sons' friends. Know who your son's friends are, who their parents are, and how to reach them. Gather phone numbers, and communicate to other parents any rumors or evidence you might find of drug use, parties at homes where adults won't be around or won't be supervising, or any other suspicious activity. Teen drinking and drug use requires both secrecy and opportunity. If you eliminate both, you're greatly reducing the chances and the inclination for teens to drink and use drugs.

The Scary Side of Pot

While many parents who grew up in the 1960s and 1970s may consider pot a mild drug that only leads to lethargy and the munchies, the marijuana on the street today is much more powerful and dangerous. A recent study of the effects of marijuana on teens and young adults found that smoking pot increases the risk for psychosis in young people. The study, conducted by researchers at Maastricht University, found symptoms such as hallucinations, delusions, and schizophrenia to be far more common among pot smokers than among non-users. A study published in 2002 in the *British Medical Journal* found a link between early pot use and an increased incidence of schizophrenia later on in life and another study in the same issue linked daily pot use with adulthood depression. Clearly, then, pot is not the benign substance so many people mistakenly believe it to be, and moms should guard against it as strenuously as other, "harder" drugs.

Signs of Drug and Alcohol Use in Teens:

- Sudden need for more privacy, locking doors, hiding things
- Change in social life, different friends, older kids, especially those unknown to parents
- Sneaking away from the house, ignoring curfews
- Slipping grades, poor attendance, discipline issues in school
- Lying about where he has been, or who he has been with

- Frequent minor illnesses, stomach issues, headaches, nausea
- Lack of attention to grooming and caring for self
- Change in eating habits, weight changes
- Stealing from family or frequent requests for money, or valuable objects disappearing, like "lost" CDs, iPods, or cell phones
- Change in sleep patterns, more or less, or sleeping at odd hours
- Odd behavior, such as being violent, threatening, depressed, jittery, too talkative, hyperactive, or spaced out

Teens, Depression, and Suicide

Teen suicide has risen dramatically in recent decades. Boys are at far more risk of suicide than girls, and sadly, boys far more often succeed in killing themselves due to the drastic and violent means they choose. According to records compiled by the Centers for Disease Control, nearly half a million teens make a suicide attempt every year, and suicide is the third leading cause of death among high school students. It's every mother's worst nightmare, and something too few of us are willing to really consider regarding our own children. It's just too painful to contemplate. But moms have to be clear-headed and proactive in examining their son's behavior and taking action.

Parents too often make the mistake of thinking *it's only a phase*, or *he's just being dramatic*, or *he's just looking for attention* when a child speaks of suicide or seems depressed and hopeless. But you *must* take it seriously. Don't make the fatal error of thinking your child could not be suicidal. Even if you think you're overreacting, even if it seems like your child's mood shifts and changes every five minutes, don't hesitate to get help. Run, don't walk, to a reliable mental health professional. If you must, any emergency room is equipped to handle this crisis, and even the local police can intervene if your son won't accompany you willingly. Even if your son is protesting he doesn't want help, threatens to run away, or otherwise tries to resist, you must get him help. If he's in this state of mind, he's unable to make rational decisions for himself, and you must make them for him. An intake psychiatrist at a hospital can force an admission to a behavioral medicine unit if your son is uncooperative and appears to be a risk to himself. If that sounds drastic, consider the alternative. It may be the hardest thing you'll ever do, but it's also the bravest, and the most important.

Symptoms of Suicide Risk:

- Drug use
- Existing diagnosed conditions such as depression, bipolar disorder, anxiety, schizophrenia, or borderline personality disorder
- Change in appetite
- Weight changes, either up or down
- Sleep pattern changes, either not sleeping or wishing to sleep all the time
- Isolation, not seeing friends or family, lack of interest in interacting
- Loss of interest in what were normally enjoyable activities
- Declining grades, poor school performance, discipline problems/disruptive behavior in class
- Lack of attention to personal hygiene and grooming
- Lack of interest in life, feeling life isn't worth living, not caring about anything, boredom, difficulty concentrating or focusing, mental confusion
- Difficulty accepting or hearing praise, thanks, getting rewards or special attention
- Feelings of worthlessness, feelings of guilt or responsibility for problems

- Feeling no one loves him or cares about him
- Sadness, thoughts of death and dying, thoughts of suicide
- Irritability, anxiety, changes in behavior, becoming aggressive, destructive
- Giving away personal items
- Frequent vague illnesses, like headache, stomachache, pain, fatigue

■ For more information on mental health issues, including teen depression and suicide, check out the National Alliance on Mental Illness at *www.nami.org*. To find a referral to a mental health professional, you can contact Mental Health America at *www.nmha.org* or in an emergency, phone them at 1-800-273-8255 to be connected to a local 24-hour crisis center. And of course, you can always call 911 to have help dispatched to your home.

Sometimes it may feel that raising a teen is like riding an out-of-control rollercoaster, up one minute, down the next, never knowing what is coming at you next. It's sometimes thrilling, sometimes frightening. But with proper information, support, and active, loving involvement in your son's life, you'll be prepared to do the very best job a mom can do.

As a Mom of a Remarkable Boy, you

- Understand that the teen brain is changing and developing, and that because of this, your son may need more help and guidance with decisions, organizational skills, and reasoning;
- Stress that sex is truly best in the context of a committed, caring relationship;

- Develop strong, open networks with other mothers to share information and guard against dangerous or unhealthy situations, both physical and emotional;
- Educate your son about the dangers of drugs, and are alert to the signs of drug and alcohol use;
- Learn to recognize the signs of depression and the warning signs of suicidal thoughts, and are proactive in seeking professional help for your son at the first sign of a problem; and
- Realize that even if your son is beginning to look more like an adult, he really is still a child, and he continues to need loads of nurturing, affection, guidance, and mentoring.

CHAPTER 5

What Defines a Family?

For the first time in contemporary American history, the traditional nuclear family of a married mother and father and one or more children actually comprises less than a majority of households. The latest U.S. census press releases available at this writing, based on 2005 population studies, counted 12.9 million single parents living with their children, with 10.4 million being single mothers, and an additional 672,000 unmarried grandparents acting as caregivers for their grandchildren. Single mothers are redefining the face of the American family, and they're bringing an ever-expanding range of family types into the American consciousness. In fact, in a recent Harris poll commissioned by *Redbook* and Lawyers.com, 99 percent of respondents said they felt families have changed compared to a generation ago.

Many single mothers raising children without a father in the home are seeking to define for themselves what a family is, and some are struggling with the feeling they aren't providing a true, complete family for their child. They may wrestle with feelings of inadequacy or guilt that are sometimes reinforced by otherwise well-meaning outsiders. Schools, churches, and social groups are often less than completely prepared to cope with an untraditional family. But there is an increasing awareness of the changing face of the American family, and while some experts still maintain the conviction that only a nuclear family unit can be successful, a growing body of mental health and child psychology professionals have begun to rethink what a child needs, and what type of home environment best meets those needs.

Accepting the New American Family

There can be resistance in trying to change the perception that the only acceptable family structure is that of a mom, dad, and the kids, all living under one roof. In a paper by University of Utah School of Medicine Professors A. Dean Byrd and Kristen Byrd, presented at the Twelfth World Conference of the International Society of Family Law in 2005, the authors contend that "Children have the best chance of developing healthy sexual identities when they are raised by both a same-sex and an opposite-sex parent. Boys and girls form their notions of sex roles from their association with both genders," and they further insist, "Supplanting the traditional family structure and replacing it with a family structure according to the individual desires wherein the role of one or more of the biological parents in the child's life is intentionally reduced or eliminated portends negative consequences in the development of the child and his or her likeliness of living a satisfying life."

Yet, at the same time, research performed by Louise Silverstein, a Yeshiva University psychology professor and co-founder of The Yeshiva Fatherhood Project, refutes this conclusion. In *Deconstructing Fatherhood*, written with Carl Auerbach, the authors contend that raising good children isn't dependent upon either having a mother or a father, per se, as long as that child has one adult completely committed to the welfare of that child, providing for the child's emotional, physical, and financial needs.

Considering the Multi-Generational Family

Many single moms have found it either necessary or desirable to live with their own parent or parents, at least temporarily, while raising children as a single parent. The stability, economic security, and presence of other adults in the home can be a tremendous boon to a young boy. In fact, a study by Thomas DeLeire and Ariel Kalil of the Harris Graduate School of Public Policy Studies of the University of Chicago titled *Good Things Come in Threes: Single-Parent Multigenerational Family Structure and Adolescent Adjustment*, found that teenagers living in a multi-generational home actually had developmental outcomes as good, and in some cases, even better, than teens living in a traditional nuclear family. This, again, supports the belief that it's not necessary to have a traditional nuclear family structure for boys to thrive, as long as their environment is stable and they have loving, supportive adults in the home.

Redefining Family

A single mother needs to have a large circle of adults that she can draw on for support, advice, and companionship. A boy, too, needs a support network. Without the large extended family of previous generations to draw upon for role models, companionship, and guidance, a boy needs a different definition of family to meet his needs in a changing society.

> "My thought on family is that 'Love makes a family' and not how the family is made up, whether single parent, gay couples, or a traditional marriage. That is the message that I am going to try to teach to my son."
>
> —*Eileen, single mom of one son*

Peggy Drexler, author of *Raising Boys Without Men*, coined a new term, the "collected family," to define the associations that defy the bounds of blood and marriage, to include those people who are brought into our lives less formally, but still as vitally.

Drexler draws a comparison between the collected family of today and the larger, extended group of people living, working, and sharing together common to earlier America. She finds this a distinct advantage to a young boy in a home without a father, since the child can draw form so many others around him for love, shared interests, and even, if necessary, discipline. Rather than relying solely on the mother for everything (a role too large for even the most competent mother to fill!), there's a variety of people with different talents and personalities for the child to learn from and grow from. In Chapter 7, we'll discuss further how to build this non-kin extended family for you and your son, using friends, mentors, and others.

Helping Your Son

Children hate to feel different from their peers, and that includes feeling that their family is somehow odd or different, particularly if they have to endure any teasing or exclusions because of their family status. If your community or your child's peer group seems to have a dearth of non-traditional households, it's important to seek out examples to help balance your child's perception. Join clubs and organizations that are either exclusively for single mothers, or that you know have a more balanced representation of family among their members, and create social events that include the children so that your son will have more opportunity to socialize with kids whose family more closely reflects your own.

It's also important to educate your school or sports clubs and Scout troops if they seem to somehow be excluding non-traditional families. Meet with your son's teacher and school staff to explain your family structure, and include other people vital to your son's upbringing, like a grandfather, uncle, or non-related caregiver in on school meetings, parent-teacher nights, and other events. Ask that father-son activities be expanded to include other family members or even close family friends. School projects related to family, such as creating a family tree or creating a collage to depict family, should affirmatively invite expansive definitions of family. The most interesting and intriguing families are often the most difficult to define!

Expanding the definition of family can be a distinct advantage in situations where a traditional nuclear family is not or cannot be available. By presenting your son with an expansive concept of family and the belief that he belongs to and is cared for by a large number of people and giving him a strong sense of connectedness, whether by blood or by sheer love and affection, you can combat the isolation and loneliness that often afflict children of single mothers.

Strengthening the Bonds of Family

Single moms should encourage strong family relationships and foster interaction between generations and with more distant relatives. One method of keeping your son aware of family is either to plan or to attend a family reunion with your child. Family reunions are growing in popularity as the population finds itself living far-removed from relatives, and they can range from something as simple as a dinner for twelve at a restaurant to elaborate days-long gatherings of hundreds at a park or large hotel. Families often choose to host their reunions at locations like Disneyland, a beach town, or even a cruise ship to give family members lots to do and to act as incentive to lure as many as possible! But just as many reserve pavilions at state parks and plan baseball games, barbecues, and "Family Olympics." The options are limited only by your imagination. If you can, help build your son's interest in advance by involving him in the planning, helping to scout locations on the Internet, and planning activities young people would enjoy. The most successful family reunions are planned many months in advance in order to allow attendees to schedule breaks from work and other obligations.

■ Check out *www.family-reunion.com* for advice and help in planning your reunion.

You can also make extra efforts to invite family members along to special events and for family dinners. Resurrect the tradition of the big family Sunday dinner, whether your family includes grandparents, aunts and uncles, or friends, both single and married with children. Keeping family strong also helps your child battle the sway of peer influence, and studies have shown that frequent contact with family reduces antisocial behaviors later on in adolescence and early adulthood.

You can also plan a family vacation that will include cousins or other family members, and don't overlook opportunities to include family members (including those non-kin family members you've collected!) in your daily life. Send our invitations to school awards nights, let everyone know when your son's soccer games are, and don't forget the band concerts! You'll build your son his very own cheering section, which can do amazing things to boost a boy's self-esteem!

Create family traditions of your own. Whether it's something simple like pizza and movie night together every Wednesday, or an annual trip to a significant location, your child will come to appreciate and treasure those moments. Those family traditions help cement and unify a family, no matter how untraditional the family may be!

Encourage an exploration of the family's history. Learning where a family came from, and what type of people the earlier generations were, can be fascinating for a child and is an excellent opportunity to teach valuable lessons regarding courage, perseverance, and problem solving by studying the example of earlier generations. This is also a great opportunity for a road trip to see places significant to your family's history, and road trips are usually marvelous chances to talk to your son free of distractions and competing entertainment.

How Media Can Help

Modern media has actually been at the forefront of expanding the accepted definitions of family, and it's a great place to talk about what makes a family. While the media is often, and justifiably, blamed for promoting some unsavory ideals, there are quite a few positive examples in the media that invite discussion and help reinforce for your son that families come in all shapes, sizes, and descriptions.

In the 1960s, TV shows often depicted children being raised by either a single, widowed parent or other adult like an uncle, with other adults living in the household to help provide support and run the home. *It's a Man's World* depicted an orphaned pair of brothers (one an adult) living together with two male friends on a houseboat and being, for each other, a family. In the 1970s, the wildly popular series *Maude* featured Bea Arthur playing the oft-married and divorced title character, living with her fourth husband and her divorced daughter, Carol, and Carol's young son, Philip. The series dealt openly with the vital issues of abortion, depression, racial guilt, and alcoholism among the principal characters and reflected the strong feminist ideals of the era. In the 1980s, *Kate and Allie* presented an entirely new dynamic of two divorced women and their children sharing a home and the responsibilities to provide better financial stability, mutual support, and a much-wanted second parent for the kids. Americans, both adults and kids, loved the depiction of successful, inventive single moms creating a happy alternative family. Later that decade, we were introduced to *Full House*, where a dad, his brother-in-law, and a close family friend banded together to raise three motherless girls.

The 1990s brought us *Murphy Brown*, whose decision to have a baby as a single mother by choice launched a national debate that reached the White House. The newer series *The Gilmore Girls* presents a single mother who gave birth as a teen and who has an extremely close and loving relationship with her daughter.

By watching and discussing TV shows that depict non-traditional families in a positive fashion, and by drawing parallels to real life families you and your son know, you can help make your son aware of the prevalence of other types of families and to expand his own, internalized definition of what's necessary to be a family.

As a Mom of a Remarkable Boy, you

- Present a broad and expansive definition of family;
- Strive to present your son with many different types of family units;
- Work to keep family ties strong for the sake of your son through meaningful exchanges, family reunions, and frequent communication; and
- Educate others in the many types of families, and model understanding and respect for all.

CHAPTER 6

Smashing the Father-Figure Myth

Even when we've conquered the issue of gaining recognition and acceptance for the single mother-led family, the moms themselves are frequently still fighting another battle, this one with themselves. Many single moms worry that by raising sons without a father in the home, they're depriving their sons of something necessary and vital. They fear that without a father around to provide a continual male element, boys will be more likely to be homosexual. Moms have also been warned that by being too involved with their sons, they'll create a man who'll be unable to have happy and satisfying relationships with women. They've been told only a father can provide crucial role modeling in channeling aggression, creating a work ethic, and becoming a successful father. But is there any basis in fact for these fears? Or can a mother raise a son without a father in the home just as successfully as a two-parent couple?

One woman I spoke to, Debbie, has been a single mother to one son for over twelve years and related this advice: "I have never discounted the role of a father in parenting—and I had wanted the perfect scenario for myself. Despite that fact, I have done a good job parenting my son as a mother and father figure. I play sports with him, and play games, and roughhouse/tickle him—which are many of the things I see other fathers do with their kids. We have camped and hiked and done many outdoor activities.

I think all children need parenting, which would include both mothering and fathering. But let's face it—more than half of our youth have single parents—so we have to be the best *one* parent that we can be, and be ever mindful of that fact.

Have confidence in yourself and your ability to do this and make it work! I have found great strength (and great rewards) in raising my son alone.

Single parenting is a lot better than people give it credit for! You have the final say-so on all aspects of raising your child (you can always get outside advice if needed, but you can make all the decisions). The child gets more of your time and attention since you do not have to balance the needs of a spouse and the children. My children mean everything to me and are the best thing that I have ever done in my lifetime!

The downside is sometimes it's tough to know the right answer on discipline, and sometime it's difficult to be consistent with kids. I am more relaxed and patient and forgiving than I would be if there were other adults and children in the family. Financially it is more difficult too.

I have great pride and great strength from doing it alone, and I feel my child also has some of that strength and confidence!"

Father Hunger

In 1980, psychiatrist James Herzog wrote a paper titled "Sleep Disturbance and Father Hunger in 18-to-28-Month-Old Boys" and spawned a huge and ongoing debate on the concept known as "father hunger." Herzog noted that the male babies he was observing were experiencing night terrors in the period following the divorce of their parents and the subsequent absence of their fathers. The children's terrors centered on fears of violence against them and needing rescue, and Herzog concluded the terrors were the result of the absence of the father. Already at that time, on many levels, American society had begun to recognize that men were experiencing an emptiness and sense of longing and regret regarding their relationships with their own fathers, and Herzog's work resonated with many in the mental health community.

Herzog followed up more recently with a book published in 2001 entitled *Father Hunger*, where the author argues that boys require closeness with their fathers in order to confidently develop their own masculinity. Herzog believes that people experience a longing for a father figure, and more specifically, that this figure acts to help formulate responses to aggression and dealing with trauma. Since then, other professionals have examined father hunger in a much broader scope, with intriguing conclusions.

One possibility that seems to be overlooked in examining the night terrors experienced by Herzog's subjects is that the children's nocturnal stress may have actually been caused by the conflict between the parents that led up to the divorce, and perhaps a fear of the father himself or a general insecurity springing from observing conflict. Other studies of children of divorce have shown that most of the emotional trauma and problems experienced by the children actually arise out of the conflict between the parents prior to the divorce, not by the divorce itself or the changed family circumstances, and those problems typically fade over time.

In an article titled "Father Hunger" published in the January/February 2003 issue of *The Therapist*, psychologist Charlyne Gelt defines the "hunger" as a need for a figure who is a "steadfast, focused, goal-directed, and compassionate guide for young males." The lack of such a guide is a growing problem in our society, according to Gelt, filling our prisons with angry, confused young men, but she attributes this problem to males growing up without boundaries and without a sense of family values and self, not to the lack of a biological father in the home precisely. Gelt feels that the shift in focus inside the family to material gain, with two working parents, leaves parents with little energy to invest in the family's emotional needs, and a shift in society away from growing a sense of community and interdependence is what is creating this tremendous void inside young men. The parents are present, but not engaged, and not providing the structure, discipline, guidance, and nurturing that the boys require.

Another article, also titled *Father Hunger*, by author of *Healing the Masculine Soul*, Gordon Dalbey, speaks of a "father-wound," a pain that even adult men suffer from a lack of closeness with their fathers, even those fathers who were present but who were simply emotionally distant and uncommunicative. Is the problem, then—the father hunger—really due to a father who is absent, or more to the lack of a male figure who cared, talked, participated, and loved? Does the trouble really then lie at the feet of generations of men who were never made to feel comfortable telling their sons "I love you," who were raised to believe their role and their worth was determined by their income and not their presence, and who themselves lacked any closeness with their own fathers? If so, what can moms do to change the course of male relationships for their own sons, so that boys can grow up to have deep, meaningful, and satisfying relationships with their own families?

Dalbey takes the encouraging approach of advocating men father themselves and each other, build a community of support, and communicate with each other, honestly and openly. We, as single mothers, can provide for our sons the tools they need to build that male community, to learn to communicate, and to stop the legacy of pain and emotional absence. In fact, single moms may be at an advantage in this.

The Importance of Male Mentors

As noted earlier in this book, a study performed on the impact of participation in Big Brothers showed that fatherless boys who had Big Brother mentors actually had experienced a lower degree of feelings of parental rejection than boys from traditional two-parent households. Because the fatherless boys had a caring adult male mentor who had specifically chosen to involve himself in the boy's life, they experienced those feelings of acceptance and the boost in self-esteem lacking in boys who had fathers present but not fully engaged in their lives, or with whom the boys were in conflict.

IT'S ABOUT PARENTING: NOTES FROM DR. HALL

Studies seeking to lay a teenage boy's problems at the doorstep of fatherless homes have missed the point. A teenager standing on the threshold of adulthood is keenly aware of the heavy load of adult responsibilities that are but a few years away. Yet, he knows that he has few tools to manage those responsibilities. Hence, teenagers need guidance and someone to help them better understand their looming responsibilities and to help equip them with the skills and information needed to meet them. Merely having a father in the picture is not enough. A hard-driving father who demands that his son become this or be that is not helpful. Nor is a father who is in the home in name only, even if he happens to be a good provider. Helping a teenager through this transition is not about gender. It's about good parenting.

Often, in a two-parent household, the father is the only adult male with whom the son has any real degree of interaction. But as Henry Ricciuti of Cornell University noted in his study on school-readiness of the children of single moms, children of single-parent homes may have many more males involved in their daily lives, such as maternal grandfathers and uncles in the household. Having many role models available is a tremendous advantage to the boys, and they can pick and choose the traits they wish to emulate, and can find support, guidance, and nurturing from many sources. And, as Peggy Drexler found in her study of sons of single mothers detailed in her book, *Raising Boys Without Men*, the boys themselves become extremely resourceful in finding male role models!

So clearly lack of a father in the home doesn't mean a boy cannot have the male figures in his lives that he needs and can learn from. In fact, historically, young men have had a number of adult male mentors in their lives, guiding them emotionally, spiritually, and professionally. It was only with the advent of the nuclear family that a boy's community of available males dwindled, and in many cases with fathers too preoccupied or too distant to be truly engaged, those male support systems completely disappeared. It's really this sense of community, the sense of "We," as Charlyne Gelt calls it, that boys are lacking today.

Many experts today conclude it takes more than just a nuclear family to provide the community a boy needs to successfully make the transition into fulfilling adulthood. Beyond just the family that lives in the home, a boy is also formed by his second-tier interactions with more distant family, other adults involved in his upbringing, and his mentors such as teachers and counselors. Further, there is another circle of influence and information provided by the child's community as a whole, including the government and the media. Each of these must be drawn upon, and must be helpful and supportive of the boy and of family as a whole, in order for the child to succeed. Depending upon Mom and immediate family only is never enough. Studies have shown that having just one good adult friend outside the family can be a significant preventative of juvenile crime.

Over and over, professionals working with children are finding that the nuclear family alone simply isn't enough to provide for the emotional needs of children. Thankfully, the need for caring adult mentors and community support for young men is being recognized and met by groups, by school, and by caring individuals taking the initiative. Programs like Team Focus, founded by Mike Gottfriend, an ESPN sports analyst and former NCAA football coach, reach out to fatherless boys through summer camps and other activities to teach leadership skills and guidance, as well as to create ongoing relationships with mentors. More information on Team Focus can be found a *www.Mike Gottfriend.net*. We will discuss where to find responsible, involved role models more in Chapter 7.

Smother-Love

While single moms are affirmatively working to provide their sons the male guidance and support the boys need, and recognize that "'it takes a village to raise a child," they often face pressure to reduce their own role in boys' lives and pull away from growing sons. On the flipside of Herzog's father hunger lies the concept of "smother-love," the idea that an overprotective, overbearing, overly involved mother will smother her son and prevent him from developing normally.

The notion of oppressive, restrictive mother love began with Sigmund Freud, who posited that a mother must withdraw from her son in order to allow the boy to bond with and identify with the father. Mothers who didn't do this were causing irreparable harm to their sons, and generations of mothers worried they were too close, too loving, too involved with their sons. Even now, you'll find mothers pushing their sons away, admonishing them to act like "big boys."

Thankfully, the vast majority of professionals have reversed the view and now teach that a close, loving relationship between a mother and a son is extremely beneficial, and that a withdrawal of affection or closeness is actually quite harmful. Of course, that doesn't apply to any parent who affirmatively fosters an unhealthy dependence either of the child on the mother, or the mother on the boy! Boys need to experience independence while still knowing they're loved and supported. Rest assured, no amount of love, affection, nurturing, and support is ever going to be harmful to a boy.

The Biological Basis for Homosexuality

The other common concern that single mothers often share is that boys lacking a father in the home might be more likely to grow up to be homosexual. Naturally, anyone would have to reason that if growing up without a father would result in the son becoming homosexual, the dramatic increase in single mother homes would have led to a sharp rise in the number of homosexual males. But this simply hasn't happened. Regardless, the myth persists and is widely promoted by certain conservative and reactionary segments of the population (often the same ones that attack single motherhood as the bane of society), and single moms have to wrestle with it. Even mothers who are quite comfortable and accepting of their gay sons recognize that their sons' lives are more challenging than those of heterosexual males, and nearly all of the moms state they would not have chosen a gay life for their child had they somehow had the choice to make. But is there really any choice at all? Is homosexuality really a matter of choice, or is it predetermined?

The nature-versus-nurture argument regarding the development of sexual orientation has undergone some dramatic shifts recently, and within the last several decades, there's been a growing body of evidence that homosexuality is at least partly determined by biology, and that people are likely just born gay.

Any observer of animal life is aware that many, many species exhibit some same-sex mating preferences. In a study of sheep performed by scientists at Oregon State University, the researchers examined the brains of both heterosexual rams and rams that displayed homosexual behavior, refusing to mate with ewes and instead preferring other rams. The scientists noted that one specific region of the brain, the anterior preoptic hypothalamus, was only half as large in the homosexual rams as the same region in the brains of heterosexual rams. Is this evidence that sexual orientation is determined even before birth? And do these findings carry over to indicate biological differences in humans as well?

Brain studies of humans have revealed similar findings to those researchers discovered in rams. The hypothalamus region of the brain controls eating, drinking, temperature regulation, and sexual behavior. Just as in rams, differences were discovered in humans in the hypothalamus of homosexual males compared to heterosexual males.

Population studies in humans also support a biological basis for sexual orientation, and that it may actually be a genetic trait. Though studies performed by Alfred Kinsey decades ago had arrived at an estimate of 10 percent of the population, and this is a statistic most adults have heard, based on the 2000 U.S. Census and other studies, gay men appear to make up about 3 to 5 percent of the population. That percentage, though, runs higher in certain families, and specifically seems to run along the maternal line, indicating there's a genetic component. A 2004 study by Andrea Camperio-Ciani of the University of Padua, Italy, confirmed what other researchers had been finding, that a gay male is more likely to also have gay uncles and nephews on the mother's side of the family. Among siblings, a gay male is four times more like to have a brother who is also gay than compared to the average population. Identical male twins, too, have a higher likelihood of both being gay, with half of gay twins also having a gay brother. These facts, again, support a genetic basis for homosexuality. In fact, DNA studies have uncovered what researchers have identified as at least one "gay gene," located on the X chromosome. Since boys must receive their X chromosome from their mother (since they receive their Y from their father), this would explain why the trait is carried along the maternal side of the family.

There even seems to be evidence that in-utero hormone exposure of male fetuses may influence sexual orientation. Among brothers, boys with older brothers are more likely to be gay, and the percentage increases with each subsequent male child the mother bears, suggesting that something occurs within the womb that influences the sexual orientation of the child. The building mountain of evidence clearly supports at least a strong component of nature over nurture in the developing sexual orientation of a child.

Single moms are faced with many challenges, but they must also take some of the pressure off themselves. By relying on good judgment, maintaining a strong, close loving relationship with their sons, and developing a good network of mentors for her child, mothers can rest assured that their sons not only are not suffering from the absence of the father, but in many cases, can actually thrive because of the single mother home.

As a Mom of a Remarkable Boy, you

- Understand that your son requires strong, caring male mentors, but not necessarily a father;
- Foster a male community for your son where he will learn to have open, honest communication and build a sense of his male self;
- Refuse to be frightened by the myth of "smother-love" and openly express your warmth, love, and caring for your son and stay deeply involved in his life;
- Accept that sexual orientation is largely biological, and fight for acceptance and understanding.

CHAPTER 7

Calling in the Troops

More than anyone, single moms need a strong support network they can turn to for help, nurturing, companionship, and advice. Isolation and loneliness, and the depression that accompanies those, are both huge risk factors for single mothers who may find it difficult to find new friends, develop community contacts, and figure out how to get the help they need. But it's not only the mother who is hurt. Studies have repeatedly shown that when moms lack a proper social support network, the child's development is negatively impacted. So how do you get started?

Friends and Family

Those already closest to you should be your first tier of support, but many single moms hesitate to call on others to help out for fear of being a burden or not seeming independent enough. Get over the idea that you're supposed to be able to do it all alone! You can't be Superwoman, and it isn't healthy to try. Let those around you know what you need. They're not mind readers, and if you don't tell them you need something, they may not volunteer. They may actually hesitate to offer their unsolicited support for fear of insulting you. Be very specific about the kind of help you need. Ask for help with:

- Shopping
- Babysitting
- Getting kids ready for bed
- Meal time
- Running errands
- Household tasks

And don't think you can't ask male friends and relatives to help out, too. In fact, that's a great way to build relationships between your son and the older males he'll need for mentoring. Grandfathers, uncles, and cousins are just as able and often tickled pink to be asked to read a bedtime story or pick up your son from an activity.

> "One of my biggest reasons for my upcoming move is that my son will have more constant male role models in his life. That is really important to me since he won't have a dad."
>
> —*Eileen, single mom of one son*

If a move has taken you far from family, you might want to consider what's best for you and your child. You need to weigh whatever benefits you have in your current community against the benefits of having family nearby, and consider the possibility of a move closer to relatives, both for your own support and to meet the emotional needs of your child.

Where to Get Help

Beyond your friends and family, there are also plenty of ways you can build a brand new support network from scratch in your community. Try organizing a neighborhood babysitting cooperative or single mother's support group. If you don't know the other parents nearby, create a flyer that you can distribute through the neighborhood expressing your interest in creating a local group. You can also post a flyer on the bulletin boards at preschools, churches, libraries (the bulletin board near the children's room is a good place to post), and the YMCA or local community center.

I formed a group that met in my living room after posting a flyer at my local, friendly second-hand bookstore, and had the added benefit of finding other women who loved to read, write, and talk about books. You should follow certain caveats when creating your flyer, of course. Don't list your address or give your full name on the flyer (after all, you don't want to advertise to the world that you're a mother alone with small kids). Instead, list a secondary e-mail address, or your cell phone number. You'll probably be surprised at how many other "secret solo moms" you discover practically under your nose!

Single Mother Organization

There are also a wealth of online communities focused on the needs of single mothers. Filled with helpful articles, links to resources, and message boards, they provide sites where single moms can chat, give advice, and support each other. A great place to start your online support network is by visiting the official site of the National Organization of Single Mothers, Inc., at *www.singlemothers.org.*

You can also join the International Moms Club (*www.moms club.org*), which not only offers a newsletter and online community, but also has chapters in most communities providing meetings and activities where moms and their kids can get together and forge new friendships. Many chapters are deeply involved in the community and participate in charities and other local organizations, further helping moms to build a sense of community and support. Kids benefit, too, by expanding their own social network and by participating in events. Originally started to handle the needs of stay-at-home mothers, Moms Club has now expanded to meet the needs of part-time and full-time working mothers, and are open to any mom seeking the support of other moms.

Hiring a Helping Hand

You may find yourself thinking you simply don't have time to do anything for yourself. Again, you need to remember the importance of taking care of yourself so that you can care for your child, and that may mean hiring help. Check with your local high school, church, and civic organizations to see if they have a "rent-a-kid" list, and contact your local continuing education department to advertise for students taking the babysitting courses many offer. These kids may even come with a training certification and education in first aid. You can find local kids eager to work at a range of chores, like yard work, dishes, or even just picking up after the kids. Even if you only hire a teenager to come in to help you around the house a few hours a week, the benefits will be amazing.

"I did not have reliable friends or family to depend on, so a lot of my child care needs were served by day-care and after-school programs. I served on the board of one day-care and one after-school program to be involved and to help shape the programs. We were able to save one from being scrapped and turned it over to our new YMCA! I also hired a co-worker's daughter to help with a week or so in summer and her son also helped out for simple events for a few hours."

—*Debbie, single mom of one son*

If you find yourself thinking, "I can't afford to hire help! I'm barely making the bills as it is!" then consider whether you ever find yourself opting to buy fast food meals because you simply don't have time to cook with so much else to do, or if you ever find yourself paying late fees on bills because you were so overwhelmed that you forgot to sit down and write out the checks on time. Could hiring a mother's helper for four hours a week twice a week allow you to do your shopping, bill paying, meal planning and cooking, and errands in a way that will actually save you money? You should also consider what you could be doing with the time you're freeing up by having a little extra help. Could you be taking an online college course to advance your career or build new skills? Perhaps you'd just use the time to have fun with your child or do something for yourself. Overwork and stress carry their own costs, in your health and personal well-being. It's estimated that half of all missed work days are somehow related to stress. Finally, consider if you could find a way to make the hired help cost less or even nothing at all!

For a while during my years in college as a young mother with small children, I swapped free room and board with another student from the university for a set number of hours of child care each week. There were quite a few education and nursing students who were looking for economical living arrangements, so I was able to interview quite a few to find the perfect match for our family. The situation benefited all of us, and it really didn't cost me much other than use of a bedroom and meals for one extra person. It meant bunking my three children into one bedroom, but it made our lives so much easier, so it was well worth it for all of us. Considering that the National Association of Child Care Resource and Referral Agencies quoted the average cost of full-time child care for a single child at more than $9,000 a year in some states, I felt the live-in part-time au pair relationship was a wonderful (and economical) solution to my child-care needs. In addition, with the flexible hours I could use (we could change the hours as often as we needed, with some in the morning and some in the evening, provided there weren't scheduling conflicts), the arrangement allowed me to do things I would otherwise have found it difficult to accomplish.

Other moms creatively barter for what they need. Perhaps you're a bookkeeper and can help someone with their household budget in return for someone to mow your lawn. Or you might be a talented seamstress who could create a prom dress in exchange for a set number of babysitting hours.

Other moms have discovered that in many cases, it costs them no more to have a private nanny or sitter providing child care in their homes compared to using a child-care center, especially if they have more than one child. The added benefit is that many sitters are able and willing to spend part of the time, such as when the children are napping or playing quietly alone, to do some light housekeeping.

Check Out the Y

The YMCA (Young Men's Christian Association) is open to people of all faiths, and isn't limited to men. In fact, it can be a mom's best ally. With facilities that provide day care, after-school programs, sports programs, health programs, and sometimes even single moms groups, the Y is a lot more than just a gym. It's also a great place to look for support for yourself and your entire family!

There are currently more than 2,600 YMCAs with more than half a million volunteers and more than 20 million members, nearly half of those children under the age of eighteen. No matter what you're looking for for your son, yourself, or your whole family, you'll likely find it at a Y!

Tim Bartlett, Executive Director of the Bridgeport, Connecticut YMCA, explains, "We're the nation's largest day care provider, and there's even financial aid for families that qualify. It's reassuring for a mom to be able to go to work after dropping her child off, knowing she has quality child care available at an affordable price."

The Y offers a number of opportunities for kids to interact with positive adult mentors and role models, too. "We've got coaches, camp counselors, even folks to help kids get started on their work lives," Bartlett says. Bartlett's Bridgeport Y even offers a special teen night, where kids can get together with their friends in a safe, supervised environment to swim, play ball, or just hang out in the community room and talk. "We even had volunteers there to help kids put together resumes for job applications," Bartlett explains. "Teen night can be a really popular event."

Teen programs abound at the Y and focus on teens developing relationships with adult mentors and with other kids. The offerings range from teen leadership programs, such as the Model United Nations, to helpful tutoring centers, junior high after-school programs, and youth employment programs.

Moms shouldn't assume that a limited family budget will preclude them from joining a Y. Just the opposite! Membership in a Y, and access to all its facilities and fantastic programs, are available on a sliding-scale fee based on family income. "Assistance can range anywhere from 0 percent to 100 percent," explains Bartlett. "Inability to pay will never keep a family from benefitting from the services of the YMCA." And that includes sports programs like soccer teams, swimming, after-school programs, even sleep-away summer camp!

The Y also offers lots of opportunities for mothers and sons to share activities and grow closer. The Adventure Guides is a Y program that allows parents and kids to spend quality time together doing exciting activities like camping. "Our focus is on building stronger families. If you have this time marked out for this activity with your child, nothing will get in the way of that." The supportive group camping offered by Adventure Guides is also a great start for camping novices, so even if you're not an old hand in the woods, you and your son can go camping with confidence as part of the Adventure Guides.

Not all programs are offered at all YMCAs, so check online to see what's available at those in your area. Visit *www.ymca.net* to get started.

Big Brothers

Big Brothers Big Sisters (BBBS) is a marvelous organization that provides one-on-one youth services, matching fatherless boys (the "Littles") with adult male volunteers (the "Bigs") for mentoring, fun activities, and supportive relationships that often last an entire lifetime. Their success record speaks for itself. Studies of boys involved in the Big Brothers program, such as those mentioned earlier in this book, have concluded that the participation has resulted in improvement in academic performance, improved self-esteem, greater social adaptation, and reduced incidence of juvenile delinquency among youth. And moms are taking advantage of the program in record numbers. BBBS has been around for nearly a century and grew by 20 percent last year alone.

Laura Green, president and CEO of Nutmeg Big Brothers Big Sisters, explained how the program worked. "We're looking to provide mentors to children who are lacking the support of an on-going connection with their other parent," she stated, "and there are no qualifications for the children. They simply need to be between the ages of six and fourteen at the time there is an application made. Our 'Littles' range from kids in some of the wealthiest suburbs to kids in some of the poorest cities. I think that's an important and unique aspect of our program."

Green explained, "The relationship between a parent and a child is so very complicated on so many different levels. It's helpful for both the parent and the child for the 'Little' to have someone to talk to, someone to seek advice from." Many of the single moms I've spoken with feel that involving their sons in

Big Brothers was the best decision they'd made for their son's welfare.

> "My son has a Big Brother through Big Brothers Big Sisters of King County. That's the primary step I've taken to providing him with male role models, and I applied for the Big Brother as soon as my son was eligible. My son likes to hang out with him. Sam's Big Brother is a man that Sam can do things with, and Sam knows he can talk about boy stuff with him."
>
> —*Jamie, single mother of one son*

There's an application process that begins with a very general gathering of demographic information such as name, address, phone number, and amount of contact with the absent parent. From there, BBBS plans a personal visit at the family's home, the mother's workplace, or the BBBS office, depending on the mother's preferences. At that time, mom and child are interviewed separately. The individual interviews allow the mother to express on her own what her concerns for her child are and what the child's history is from her perspective without embarrassing the child. She can also discuss her ideals and goals about the program as they pertain to her child. The mother gets to express what characteristics she'd be looking for in a Big Brother for her child.

Then the staff sits down with the child, who can tell them what his interests are and what activities he'd like to do with a Big Brother. The interviewer can also gauge how excited the child is about participating in the program.

Volunteers come from all walks of life. The minimum age to be a Big Brother is eighteen, but Green has seen volunteers as old as seventy. "Most of our volunteers are coming from suburban communities," Green said, "and they've generally been between twenty-five and thirty-five. They're usually upwardly mobile professionals who want to give back to the community."

"We run two types of programs," Green continued. "One is a school-based program where the 'Bigs' and 'Littles' meet at school only during the school day or after school. We also offer our best-known community-based program where the 'Big' and 'Little' design their own activities and go off into the community. We also have high school students who are involved in mentoring elementary school students in various school systems, and we've even had instances where we have upperclassmen mentoring middle school students about the enter high school."

"Before we actually make a match," Green explained, "we gather the same kind of information about the Big that we gather from the parent. What are your interests? What do you feel are the characteristics in a child that you would feel comfortable or uncomfortable working with? Then we take those children's applications and interviews and the Big Brother applications and try to figure out who makes the most sense to fit together. We then talk to the Big and give a synopsis of the child without giving a name, and call the mom and tell her we have a Big with the following characteristics and at this point she can say yes or no to the match." If both agree, there will be a four-way meeting between the mom and her son, the potential Big Brother and the staff at BBBS. Everyone gets a chance to talk, and the Big and Little can draw up a list of activities they'd like to do together and then have a fifteen or twenty-minute trial run. If all goes well, a match is made!"

BBBS also maintains contact with the parent and child throughout the Big Brother/Little Brother relationship, by phone, e-mail, or in person, so they're constantly assessing the child's safety and the progress of the relationship. They also check with the volunteer about his own satisfaction with the relationship since they know that the longer a match lasts, the more powerful the impact.

The "Bigs" undergo a background check and a driving history check, and must give three references that BBBS interviews, and one reference must be the current employer. "We talk with the employer because we're seeking to find out if the person has a good history of consistency, and of maintaining relationships over time. Someone who is job-hopping is probably not a good candidate to be a Big Brother. After all, most of these kids have already experienced an abandonment, and they now need someone they can depend on."

"The average match between our 'Bigs' and 'Littles' lasts 2.8 years," Green says with pride, "and typically the reason they end at all is because one or the other moves out of the area." But even after the "Bigs" and "Littles" stopping meeting regularly, they frequently maintain a close relationship for years afterward, often well into adulthood. "We had an executive at Pratt & Whitney," Green relays, "who had been a Big Brother when he was in college and had maintained the relationship with his Little Brother for many years afterward. They were so close that when the Pratt & Whitney exec was offered a job at a competing company, the first person he called for advice was his Little Brother!"

As the Single Mom of a Remarkable Boy, you

- Realize you can't do it all alone, and involve friends and family;
- Explore the many opportunities your community offers for mentoring your son;
- Join or develop your own support groups; and
- Find creative ways to trade, barter, or hire help with baby-sitting and chores.

CHAPTER 8

Making Choices Regarding Your Own Life to Benefit Your Child

As a single mom, you're balancing a million obligations. Experts say you need to spend lots of time with your son. They also say that economic security is a key factor to your child's success. Your job might be asking you to relocate just as your child's making friends and acclimating to school. How do you possibly choose? The place to start with any major decision is by analyzing your financial situation. Everything else hinges on that. Whether you're considering if you should change your job, or even look for a brand new career, go back to school, or move to a new place, you can't really make an informed decision unless you know where you stand financially.

Establishing Priorities

As a mother, you have to provide certain absolutes for your child, and those are food, shelter, clothing, medical care, and education. Obviously, though, there's quite a range within those categories. Some moms are going to feel they need to have a college fund growing in the bank, while others are going to be content as long as they can put dinner on the table and the car isn't repossessed.

The vast majority of single mothers have no savings whatsoever. That's a frightening fact. The group that's most vulnerable is the one that's least equipped to cope with a financial downturn or emergency. Something as simple as a blown transmission on a car can have economic ripples that set the family back for years. Do you fix the car or pay the electric bill? If you pay a credit card late because the money went elsewhere, it could mean negative credit ratings, which could increase the interest rate on the loans you do have, result in denial of a housing application or home loan, or even impact your career, since many jobs now run routine credit checks on potential employees. Obviously, the first order of business to any single mom has to be establishing savings against emergencies, and in order to do that, you have to get your monthly finances under control.

If you're finding yourself constantly caught short, or you feel there's no way for you to possibly carve out any of your income to start a savings account, take a deep breath and resolve to closely examine your spending. Financial advisors recommend focusing on creating a budget that lists all your expenses and income. What do you pay first? Obviously, rent, utilities, insurance, car payments, medical expenses, and groceries are at the head of the list. But can any of those be trimmed?

The Importance of a Budget

Early Show financial expert Dave Ramsey suggested in an interview for CBS News that even if a single mom runs a budget and realizes she doesn't make enough to pay all the expenses, she'll still be in better control and can begin to analyze where expenses can be cut and really begin to get her money under control. He also advises single moms to find an "accountability partner," someone who will help you decide on expenses and hold you accountable if you go on a shopping spree. Being alone and having no one you have to show your credit card bills to can sometimes allow women to feel a little more free to indulge themselves, so find a good girlfriend or relative who can reel you in when you're tempted to go beyond your budget.

One of the biggest mistakes that moms make after divorce or separation is remaining in the same home they lived in when they were together with their child's father when they really can't afford it. While keeping things as normal as possible for your child is a great idea—and there is sometimes a tiny feeling of resentment (*I'm not going to let this divorce drive me from my home!*)—if the home is really more than you can handle, either because of the mortgage, the utilities on a bigger place, or the maintenance and upkeep, it's time to look to move to a smaller place. While at first it might seem cramped, consider how much freer you're going to feel at the end of the month when you have a few hundred extra dollars in your checkbook! Talk about breathing room! If you feel you're short-changing your child in the move, consider that the extra money can be used to start saving for your child's education, or to provide much-needed services you haven't been able to afford for him to this point. Always wanted to be able to afford a tutor but never felt you were able to? Examine costs and benefits for all of your financial decisions.

It All Adds Up

Beyond the recurring expenses you face every month, you probably spend small amounts of money throughout the week without really ever paying attention. Track your daily spending in a small notebook in your purse, and list every dime you spend. Did you drop $4 on a latte without thinking twice? Did you buy lunch when you could have brought last night's leftovers from home? Did you jump in a cab instead of walking? Did you pick up an extra magazine at the grocery counter on impulse? When you add up the small amounts of money you spend here and there, you may see it adding up quickly to a sizable amount, often enough to significantly impact your budget. Even if you can save just a small amount daily, by applying your savings either to paying down debt or to creating your emergency fund, you'll quickly work yourself into a more financially secure position.

Single moms need to become experts in frugality! By keeping track not only of your daily expenses, such as gasoline, dry cleaning, coffee, newspapers, and more regular expenses like clothing, utilities, and car insurance, you can analyze where you can begin to save money in bigger ways, too. Can switching to a new car insurance carrier save you several hundred dollars a year? Have you analyzed your health insurance policy to make certain it's the most cost-efficient one you can have?

Perhaps making a large investment now will save you money over the long term. For example, replacing an old roof may result in a lower heating bill, which would pay for the cost of the roof over about a five-year period. It also greatly enhances the look of your home, and increases its value should you decide to sell the house.

Getting a Handle on Debt

By saving just a little each day and in many ways, and directing that savings toward your debt, you will eventually become debt-free, and you'll be providing financial security for yourself and your child.

Most Americans carry thousands in credit card debt, and many barely make the monthly minimum payment. If that sounds like your situation, consider this: By only making the minimum payment, you're barely covering the finance charges for the month, and you're not chipping away at the balance. Instead, the credit card company is charging you, over and over again each month, for the "privilege" of letting you maintain that balance. If you examine what a purchase made on a credit card really costs you over the entire period of time it takes you to pay it off, including the interest, you may find you're paying twice (or more!) the cost of the item. It's not worth it to buy on plastic, especially if you're a single mom with a limited income. It's essential you eliminate your credit card debt as quickly as possible, and then stop using the cards for anything but an absolute emergency.

Determine which of your cards carries the highest interest rate or highest monthly use charges, and work on paying that one down first. If you can qualify, transfer your balances to a card that has a zero percent introductory rate. You can also call your credit card company and negotiate a lower interest rate on your existing cards. Carefully read the language on any new credit card agreement. Many sneak in language that allows them to have a default interest rate so that if you are ever late on a payment, or go over your credit limit, your interest rate automatically jumps to an astronomical figure.

If you think your credit card debt is simply too high and you've given up the dream of ever paying it off, just try seeing if you are able to scrape together just an extra $100 per month to apply towards your credit debt, and transfer your balance to a zero percent card (and keep transferring each time the introductory period ends!) so none of your payment is going toward useless interest payments. It will take time, but you'll see your balances decreasing. You have to resist the impulse to then see that available credit as money you can spend, though!

You may also consider asking your bank for a personal loan to pay off your higher-interest debt (don't be afraid to shop around!). Compare interest rates and any other fees that would be incurred in taking out the loan, and have the bank calculate the monthly payment you'd be required to pay. Since the term over which you can pay back a personal loan may be just a few years, the monthly payment may be higher than the monthly payments you're making on the credit cards, even if the interest rate is lower, so know in advance what you can afford to pay. Ask if there are different terms available.

Finally, though it may seem distasteful, consider asking a family member for a loan to get rid of your high-interest debt. If, as most single moms, you're barely making ends meet, you simply can't afford excess interest charges eating up your precious financial resources. It's in the best interests of your family to do what is needed to make your family secure.

The Importance of Insurance

You must, absolutely must, invest in a life insurance policy to protect your child, and currently, four out of ten single parents have no life insurance coverage, and most of those who do, have too little. The typical single-parent policy covers only about $60,000, while two-parent households usually hold policies to cover an average of $250,000. When you think of it, though, which family needs more protection?

When I divorced and realized that my kids might need to be able to take care of themselves on their own, I sought the advice of a financial advisor. I came up with what I liked to call my "Now, in case I get hit by a bus" plan. What are my kids going to need to know and what money are they going to need to have should I suddenly no longer be there to care for them?

He told me that, at minimum, a parent should provide for five to ten years of her regular annual income in an insurance policy. Most life insurance applicants have to take a physical to qualify. A parent, especially with younger children, would also need to consider things like paying off a mortgage or providing housing support even if relatives would be responsible for the child and what expenses they'll incur taking care of him. Would taking care of your son, no matter how much they love him, be a financial hardship on them and their other children? Would they be able to afford to send him to college? Having a life insurance policy protects everyone, not just your child.

Make multiple copies of your insurance documents and give them to each of your children, and one to your attorney. Everyone needs to know what insurance you have and whom they should contact to file a claim. Many insurance policies go unclaimed simply because no one knew they existed. You must also be sure to keep the insurance company informed about the beneficiary of your policy, and that person's (and there can be several) current contact information.

Life insurance is less expensive than one might imagine, especially if you buy term insurance. Term insurance only lasts for a set period, like ten or fifteen years, and then the policy elapses. This is a less expensive form of insurance that might suit your needs if you simply want to cover the period until your son is grown. Whole life, on the other hand, allows you to continue to maintain the policy indefinitely and actually has a cash value that you build with your payments, but it is more expensive. You should speak to an advisor to determine your needs and what you can afford.

You should also consider a disability insurance policy, especially if your job if the sole source of income for your family. Being without an income—even very temporarily—due to illness or injury can be devastating to a family, particularly if the family has little savings. Labor and employment attorney Michael Devlin suggests single moms first investigate to see whether they have a disability policy through their work. "This is separate from worker's compensation," he advises, "since this relates to non-work related injuries and illnesses." Some states also offer a uniform disability policy, so look into that as well. But if you're not otherwise covered, consider investing in a private policy that will cover you should you be unable to work. These policies can be tailored to your own financial tolerances and are typically priced very reasonably. "Generally," says Devlin, "short-term disability policies have a five-day waiting period in case of illness, and a one-day waiting period in the case of a non-work related injury, such as a car accident." Short-term disability will cover you for a period of up to six months, providing a portion of your salary, generally sixty percent to two-thirds. You can also look into a long-term disability policy, which kicks in at the six-month period and pays until retirement with certain offsets for social security disability and other payments you might receive. Finally, if you are injured at work and you're told your employer does not have worker's compensation, you should still file a claim. "Your employer will still have to pay," Devlin states, "it would just come out of their general funds."

Child Support

If you're raising a child as a single mom in America, chances are the father owes a child support obligation. And chances are, you have either not received child support or are owed an arrearage on the support ordered. In the United States, fully half of all child support cases have received absolutely no collections at all, and in some areas, such as the District of Columbia, noncompliance with child support orders exceeds 80 percent of cases. Those numbers don't even include cases where some child support is being collected, but not the full amount of the order. A great many single mothers, too, don't realize that their child's father owes them support, even if they were never married or living together. It's not a matter of the father being nice or being upstanding. It's his legal obligation.

Economic hardship is one of the key crises facing single mothers, and it's one of the leading indicators of behavioral problems in boys from fatherless homes. Without sufficient economic means, effective parenting becomes more challenging. Financial stress on the mother is often associated with defiant behavior by the child, and the stress of worrying about money alone can cause the mother anxiety and depression. The percentage of single mother households living in poverty is a national disgrace.

Some single mothers shun requesting child support from the court, or somehow feel it's a matter of pride that they don't enforce an order of support. More than one single mother I've encountered has told me regarding their children's father, "He knows where we are. If he wanted to give us something, he would." I understand the sentiment to a degree, that if a father wants to walk away from his child and his obligations as a parent, good riddance to him, and a son often fares better not having contact with a reluctant or disengaged father. However, given the choice, the majority of non-residential fathers would opt out of paying regular child support. Studies have shown that paternal involvement with children after separation or divorce drops off sharply as the years pass, and as the amount of interaction with the child ebbs, often so does the father's perception of his financial obligation to the child.

There's also a fear that obtaining a child support order (or attempting to) will create conflict with the child's father. The problem with that reasoning is that if the father of your child isn't helping to support the child now, you're already in conflict. Retired family law attorney, Brette McWhorter Sember, author of *Co-Parenting with Your Ex* and *The Divorce Organizer and Planner*, offers the following advice to moms who are reticent about enforcing court-ordered support: "Child support is not optional. It's a court order that has to be complied with. The purpose of child support is to ensure that the child has an adequate standard of living after divorce. The money is meant to better the child's life. A mother who does not enforce child support or sits back and waits for a delinquent father to pay when he can is doing a disservice to her child. Standing up and demanding what your child is entitled to is part of your responsibility as a parent. If your child's teacher decided to only teach on days she felt like it, you would be up in arms, demanding that she teach. Child support should be viewed the same way.

"Too many people think child support is something that benefits the mother. A father who pays child support is more likely to use his visitation, which means it's more likely the child will have a relationship with that father, something that research shows is extremely important. I also personally believe a father who pays child support will feel a greater connection to his child. Child support creates a relationship and a responsibility, even if it is only financial. Asking a man to honor his responsibility to his child is not being demanding, pushy, or greedy. Your child support order was decided upon and put in place by a judge. Ignoring that order is detrimental to your child's well-being. Insisting on the benefits your child is entitled to is a parent's job."

Since 1994, all orders for child support have been accompanied by a provision for an automatic wage garnishment, which takes effect immediately unless the parties agree to handle the payment of the child support in another manner. Even if you'd previously agreed to allow your child's father to pay his child support directly, you can activate the wage garnishment later on, and if an arrearage has accrued, the wage garnishment can withhold an additional amount to cover back-owed support as well as the current obligation. There are federal limits on what percentage of the father's income can be taken as a wage garnishment to meet his obligation, but since child support orders are typically based largely on the father's income, the support amount can typically be covered completely through garnishment. Obviously, if your child's father loses or quits his job and is receiving no income, no wages can be garnished. However, the law provides for the delinquent parent's tax refunds and unemployment insurance to be diverted to cover child support obligations, and his property can be seized and in some cases, his driver's license revoked for noncompliance. If you're owed child support you are not receiving, you should consult an attorney who handles family law matters.

Fortunately, you're not alone in your efforts to collect child support for your child. The Child Support Enforcement Program combines the efforts of federal, state, and local agencies to enforce child support orders, even across state lines, and by using the Federal Parent Locator Service (FPLS), state agencies can track and locate parents owing child support by tracking employment. More information on child support collection is available in the appendix at the back of this book.

Career Issues

As a single mom, you face more and more complicated decisions regarding your career. Becoming more informed about your options, and perhaps considering new possibilities, can change a limited horizon to an unlimited one!

Career Advancement or More Time at Home?

Moms are torn between their need to spend time with their children and their need to provide for them economically, and for many, this results in stagnation. Attempting a move in one direction, like advancing a career by seeking a promotion and more responsibilities in order to bring home more money, could mean taking more away from the other end of the balance, resulting in less time at home with your son. Try to devote yourself more to your child, and your career could suffer. You read that economic hardship is one of the big risk factors for behavior issues with sons of single moms. You also know that a lack of attention takes its toll. It's enough to make you pull your hair out! Which way do you turn? Perhaps the answer is in determining whether your current job is really the best one for you as a single mom.

Would a Career Change Be Right for You?

You might decide that the job you have right now is simply not the best for your current situation. If you're unhappy at your work, or your employer's too inflexible regarding the demands of single motherhood, or you simply realize there's no real opportunities for career advancement or new challenges within the company, you should at least consider the possibility of a new job. If so, consider the following options.

Family-Friendly Companies

Perhaps you're extremely happy with the type of work you do, but the company you work for isn't particularly understanding about the needs of single, working moms. It might be time to start looking around for a work place that's more suited to your needs. Some companies recognize how valuable their employees are and have developed policies that make them more family-friendly places to work. Policies like allowances for personal and sick time; flexibility in work hours (so-called "flex time"); allowances for part-time work, telecommuting, and on-site child care; and even counseling referrals all make it much more likely that a single working mother can thrive in her job. In fact, most companies offering these policies have noted that their employees have better attendance, better job satisfaction, and greater loyalty.

"I am an IT project manager for a large company. I have been really lucky that I am able to work from home when I needed. I am going to be taking a new position in the company in April (hence my move) and have recently found out that my new boss is also a single mom of a son! Therefore, she is very flexible and understanding about working remotely and various child care issues."

—*Eileen, single mom*

Flex time is interpreted differently by different companies, but typically, it allows the worker to negotiate her work hours to suit her schedule, such as starting earlier or later in the day, or compressing the workweek into four days. Naturally, not all workplaces or all jobs can tolerate schedule irregularities, but if your employer allows for flex-time, investigate how you can use it to benefit your home life. Perhaps you can start in the morning right after putting your son on the bus to school instead of waiting an extra hour-and-a-half for your workday to begin, and then be out in time to pick him up from his after-school activity. Maybe you can schedule to allow you to coach your son's soccer team, or at least to attend the later afternoon games?

Telecommuting is a wonderful option that more and more companies are finding works well, not only for the employee, but for the employer, too. Is your job one that would allow you to perform at least some of the duties from home? With technologies such as online meetings and conference calling, you're practically in the next room! Some companies will provide a computer, printer, and other resources necessary to establish a home office. The trickiest part about this, for some moms, is the lure of other things you need to do around the house interfering with your work time. You need to determine if you can discipline yourself, and teach those around you, to respect your work time and your home office.

On-site child care is a benefit that mothers absolutely love. Being able to bring your child with you to work and leave him at the nursery, and then share your lunch times and break times with him throughout the day, allows for lots of bonding and communication. Some companies even offer a nursery cam where you can check out your child in the nursery, online, as he plays, naps, and interacts with the teacher. You also then can simply pick him up on your way out, rather than having to commute to the babysitter's or day care.

Moms need to be aware of their right to take time off to cope with emergencies at home, too. The Family Medical Leave Act, or FMLA, is a federal law that allows workers who find they need time off to care for a family medical issue, such as a sick child, to be absent from a job without incurring disciplinary action or violating a minimum attendance policy. Attorney Michael Devlin explains, "Family Medical Leave doesn't provide for paid leave, but it does allow a mother to take care of a sick child without her absence being counted against her attendance at work. Notify your employer of your need for time off as soon as you're aware of it, and it's your employer's obligation to properly label it as FMLA."

Consider a Home-Based Career

Just as I did when I found myself a single mom with two school-age children, you might determine that working from home is really the most workable solution to your problems. While for many that means a lower income than one might be able to earn working outside the home, it also means fewer work-related expenses for commuting, business attire, meals outside the home, and other items. It could also reduce your child-care expenses if you can work successfully with your child at home with you some or all of the time. Many home-based businesses also offer tremendous flexibility in working hours, so you can put in hours early in the day, after children's bedtime, during naps, and on weekends.

> "I just switched from working full-time at one organization to doing freelance work on my own. I work 30–40 hours now, about half from home and about half from clients offices."
>
> —Jamie, mother of Sam

According to a study by the Independent Insurance Agents and Brokers of America, there are approximately 11 million home-based businesses in the United States right now, and statistics show that women are more successful at starting their businesses than men are. That's because women have several things going for them. They tend to research their intended business more than men do before attempting to launch, they choose businesses that require less start-up money, and they're willing to seek advice from professionals like SCORE, the Services Corps of Retired

Executives (*www.score.org*) where volunteers work with new business owners to help them be successful.

There's a growth in the type of businesses being run successfully from home, and many jobs traditionally done from an office as part of a larger firm are now being done by individuals from home. For example, much of the travel industry has moved from office-based services to home-based. The Web site *www.entrepreneur.com* has a women's center specifically devoted to female business owners and offers informative articles on such issues as micro-loans and business insurance. It's wonderful inspiration!

Another Web site for moms thinking about looking at a home-based career is *www.moneymakingmommy.com*. As the site warns, always be wary of scams and schemes that sound too good to be true.

Back to School for Mom!

Lots of moms either delayed or cut short their educations when the kids came along. Is it time now to finally finish? Whether you're considering returning to school to finish a college degree, or you're thinking of enrolling in a professional training program like culinary school, real estate, or training as a court reporter, it's a big change for the entire family and something you need to think through carefully and discuss with your son so he's aware of what it would mean. It could impact quite a number of aspects of your life, including your budget, your free time, and even vacations. However, by hitting the books yourself, you'd set a great example for your child and demonstrate how much you value learning.

If you feel going to school is simply out of the question due to finances, think twice. Community colleges and many local four-year schools are extremely reasonable. Tunxis Community College in Connecticut is typical of many two-year schools and has a per-credit tuition charge, as of Spring 2007, of $98 per credit plus a small college services fee. Full-time tuition for a semester, fees included, for a state resident is only a little over $1,300. And non-traditional, full-time returning adult students still qualify for financial aid. Whether you plan to attend a traditional college or an accredited professional training school such as a culinary institute, you need to plan ahead since there's a priority given to applications received early in competing for available money. In some cases, once it's gone, it's gone! Find out when the FAFSA (Free Application for Federal Student Aid) is due for the term and turn it in as soon as possible. Between grants and other financial aid, many lower-income students at less-expensive institutions find nearly their entire tuition bill covered, and for those who want and qualify (which is nearly everyone), there are student loan programs that provide low-interest loans for which payments don't begin until after graduation or withdrawal from school.

The Web site *www.adultstudent.com* provides an incredible list of links of interest to returning adult students, covering not only financial aid, but how to prepare to go back to school, how to take notes, and even success stories of single moms who made the leap successfully. Another great resource Web site is *www.Further YourEducation.com*, which is specifically geared to the non-traditional student.

A Web site that has proved to be helpful for many single mothers is *www.fastweb.com*. It matches students with available grant and scholarships and send information about them via e-mail, as well as e-mail reminders of upcoming deadlines for applications. Some of the scholarships are truly unique (one offered money to winning students of a "write an essay on your most hated vegetable" contest for example), and many are very off-the-beaten path, a good place for non-traditional students to look for cash for school.

Don't overlook opportunities for distance learning via online classes. You can sometimes combine online and classroom-taught classes at a single institution. You can also just go part time and take as little as a single class at a time, if that's more your speed and convenient to your schedule.

Many institutions of higher learning have family student housing available, too, which, in addition to providing reasonable-cost housing, could also surround you with like-minded adults, often with children of their own, to provide support and encouragement. For example, Snow College in Utah offers two-bedroom cottages for a fee of $375 per month, with room for a maximum of two children, and has an option to request a partially furnished cottage if you don't have everything you need to set up housekeeping. Students there must be registered for a minimum of ten credits per semester to qualify; once accepted, they pay only a minimal security deposit. Offers like this make it extremely tempting, and affordable, for a single mom to return to school.

Some employers also offer tuition reimbursement programs, particularly if the employee is going to school to gain a skill useful to the employer. Check at your workplace to see if you'd be covered. You can also discuss the possibility of a leave-of-absence from your job to further your education.

If not having a degree is holding you back, or if more education could further your career and enhance your life, don't assume your choices are limited by your situation. Make an appointment to speak to both a college admissions officer and a financial aid officer to explore your options.

Sharing a Home, Sharing the Work

As you're analyzing your needs and your family's financial situation, you might decide life would be easier if there were a second adult to share the load. But there's not always a family member available, or perhaps you just don't want them that involved in your daily life (been there, done that, never again). Consider the option of shared housing. CoAbode is a service that's helped more than 25,000 single moms raising kids on their own to locate other moms in the same situation to work together to find affordable housing they can share. Moms split rent, utilities, groceries, and child responsibilities, as well as provide companionship, support, and nurturing for each other. CoAbode reports that participants are reducing their expenses on housing by up to 55 percent, and on other expenses like food, utilities, and child care by about 40 percent. Members also feel there's a benefit in gaining time, as well as money, by sharing responsibilities, and that's time you can use to take classes, help your son with school work, or finally have time for some fun activities you've been putting off. There's a minimum cost to join, or you can just access their shared housing database for a one-time fee, and you can even apply for a free membership provided by a sponsoring business or individual. See *www.coabode.com*.

Intentional Communities

A larger scale project where singles, couples, and families might come together to share housing, costs, and responsibilities is called an intentional community. Some of these communities will remind you of the old-school communes of the 1960s, but others are simply communities where people who share a common background, like artists, or a common lifestyle goal, like organic living, come together. Some are single-sex, while others allow both men and women, and the living arrangements vary but often feature individual living spaces for families with a large common building or area for shared meals and interaction like watching TV, talking, or exercising together. As you might expect, there are intentional communities in rural farm-like settings, but you can also find them in urban settings.

Often called co-housing, the lifestyle allows for a greater sense of community. Kids living in co-housing communities get to know other adults besides their parents and have other kids who live with them like siblings. Co-housing allows for less by way of living expenses, since many things can be shared, like toys for children, garden tools, even vehicles. Food costs are usually much lower because of the shared common meals and because many of these communities have extensive gardens to help grow their own food.

Each intentional community sets its own rules and guidelines. They usually require a certain number of hours of labor from each adult participant, helping with maintenance, meals, and gardening. There's usually a fee to join, but the amount varies a good deal depending on the exact set-up of the community. If you're thinking you and your child could benefit from a co-housing situation, start by visiting Intentional Communities at *www.ic.org*.

As a Mom of a Remarkable Boy, you

- Get your family budgets under control to gain greater financial security;
- Protect your family with insurance coverage;
- Make sure that any child support obligations owed your child is paid;
- Consider changing jobs or careers if it will suit your family's needs;
- Consider returning to school to further your education; and
- Consider alternative housing arrangements.

CHAPTER 9

Discipline and the Single Mom

The single most significant change in our society over the second half of the twentieth century was the transfer of authority from the parent to the child. As a mother, you're no doubt aware of some of this going on around you, as you compare your son's generation to your own as a child, and then to how your grandparents raised your parents. Children are making decisions today on matters as far ranging as to when they go to bed, what friends they keep, how they dress, and what the family eats. At the same time, they participate and contribute less to the running of the household.

This transfer of authority has even had an impact on children's health! A surprising result of this transfer of parental authority is the rise in the number of overweight children. Where parents once strictly monitored a child's eating (do you remember your mother ordering you to drop that cookie because it would ruin your appetite?), children are now often free to eat whatever and whenever they choose. Even outside the United States, children are making a large share of the decisions on the family's meal choices. But how did this occur?

WHERE DID THE AUTHORITY GO?
NOTES FROM DR. HALL

How did it happen that parents relinquished their authority? We think it happened for two reasons. One reason is the huge shift over the last half century in the demographics of the United States. The 1950 census reported that three out of every four families either lived on a farm or worked in a small rural town whose economy was dependent on agriculture. In that day and age, the vast majority of families were nuclear, and few mothers worked outside the home/farm. Farm children started working at an early age right alongside of their parents, doing any and every job that they were physically and mentally capable of performing. As early as six years of age, the boy was responsible for feeding the chickens and gathering the eggs. Every Saturday, the family went to town where the eggs were sold, with the egg money going to buy family necessities. The boy understood that by tending the chickens, he was making a contribution to the family's livelihood. A seven-year-old girl helped her mother by folding the freshly washed clothes and setting the table for meals. As the children worked side by side with their parents, they watched their parents closely. Children saw the jobs their parents did, and they were eager to acquire the ability to do those tasks. Today, men who grew up on a farm remember the first day they drove the tractor, and women who grew up on the farm remember when they were put in charge of baking pies for the threshing crew.

When families were agrarian, an authoritarian approach to discipline worked. It worked because the critical components of the authoritarian model were in place. Of course, the most crucial component was the enforcer. For an authoritarian model to work, the enforcer must always be within sight or not far away. If children do not comply with a directive, the "or else" happens. As the adage from the time advised, "spare the rod and spoil the child." Back in those days, there were not many spoiled children. Sometimes the consequence for not following a parent's directive was worse than being spanked. A friend recently related to me a story that illustrated the point. "I'll never forget," he said, "the time Dad told me to go shut the gate at the south pasture. I didn't think it mattered whether the gate was shut or not, so I didn't do it. The next morning our cows were in our neighbor's oats. After we got the cows out of the oats, Dad told me to go tell the neighbor it was my fault and ask how much we owed him."

The authoritarian model that parents used successfully back in the fifties must be understood in its full context. In the agrarian family, children saw how Dad responded when the hay bailer broke down in the middle of haying season, they saw how mom dealt with the exhaustion of cooking for all the neighbors that came to help with the spring branding, they saw how their parents handled a dispute with a neighbor. All this they watched, and from these situations, children learned how they should handle frustration, how they should cope with their mental and physical exhaustion, and even how they should deal with interpersonal conflicts. Today, the census statistics from 1950 are reversed, and four out of five families live in an urban or suburban setting. The nuclear family is no longer at the center of the majority of households. Even if it is a nuclear family, most mothers and fathers both work outside the home. When asked what their parents do for a living, most children are unable to say more than "Mom works in a store, and Dad works in an office." Today's children have little idea what their parents do during a typical day at work. Hence, children do not get to see how their parents or other adults cope with frustration, stress, or interpersonal situations. In short, parents no longer model essential life coping skills for their children. Today's parents do not consciously relinquish authority to their children. Rather, they take jobs that require them to be away from home for most of the children's waking hours.

The other reason that the authoritarian model of discipline does not work is technology. Nearly every eight-year-old knows how to access the Internet and Google information and pictures about any word or concept that enters his mind. Most teenagers have a cell phone with their own calling circle. Children from New York City and San Francisco watch the same TV programs, listen to the same music, and play the same video games, binding them in a subculture that has a tremendous impact on their attitudes and beliefs, and that, at times, is an even more powerful influence on them than are their own parents. This, too, is a reason why the authoritarian model of discipline no longer works.

Part of this problem in relinquishing authority is that the parents attempt to relate to the child as a friend rather than a parent. They want to be the cool parents. But with that comes difficulty in being an effective authority figure. And that is something single mothers of sons absolutely must be. It is in the nature of boys to seek a leader, to want structure, rules, and a proper stratification of relationships. Even in their social circles, boys establish leaders and a pecking order. In letting them know you're in charge, you're also assuring them that they're taken care of. Boys want to know the limits, and what's expected of them. They actually crave discipline.

How Is Discipline Different from Punishment?

Too many people mistake discipline for punishment. Punishment is a punitive measure, such as spanking, grounding, withdrawing privileges, or giving extra chores. Discipline is a system of orderly living that teaches and reinforces respect, known expectations, self-reliance, and proper behavior. Discipline is used to internally instill the understandings and values that promote good behavior. A child who is disciplined is one who knows how to act and what to do. He seeks to make his parent happy, and feels good about himself for making his parent proud. Imagine a disciplined adult, and what comes to mind? A highly trained athlete whose sacrifices and hard work have brought great accomplishment? A soldier whose mind and body are honed to keep on task and respect authority, and yet who can take the lead when called upon with great competence and assurance? A disciplined child gains all those attributes and skills, and is a pleasure both to himself and to others.

Instilling Discipline

So how do you regain your authority and raise your child to be a disciplined person? As in the chapter on communication, one way a parent can immediately start to assume authority is to speak to boys in the proper tone. Rather than using a voice that attempts to plead or cajole or even explain and hope for cooperation, a mother must use a voice that brooks no argument. She must state her directive, clearly and simply, and if necessary, will provide a timetable for completion of the task. Rather than saying, "I think you should straighten your room," state, "Clean your room today." The child's not interested in hearing what you think should happen, he needs to know if he has to do it! Instead of saying "jumping off the top stair could hurt you," tell your son, "Walk down the stairs." Later on, when you're not in the middle of giving a directive, you can explain why something wouldn't

133

be a good idea, but at the moment something's happening (or about to) the child just needs to know what you want him to do. Rather than ask, "Can you take the garbage out?" say, "Take the trash out right after dinner." You've stated the directive and given the time frame in which it should happen. Leaving it an open-ended kind of question, "Can you take the garbage out?" will likely result in either the child figuring, "Yes, I could," but not doing it, or assuming there's no deadline for the task to occur, so he can do it tonight, or tomorrow, or whenever he gets around to it. Or forgets about it. Ever find yourself repeating yourself over and over and wondering what's going wrong and why your child isn't listening? Perhaps the problem is you're phrasing the directive incorrectly!

Follow the Leader

You must also be aware of the role model you're presenting when insisting on discipline with your child. Lead by good example. If your areas tend to be messy, it's hard for the child to see the need for a tidy room. If you're disorganized and constantly losing papers and paying bills late, it's hard to come off as genuine in trying to enforce order in your child's homework. If you don't pay attention to your own eating habits, you can't expect your child to be careful with his. An awful lot of parents try to rule by "Do as I say, not as I do," but that will only go so far!

Even as you should be aware of the model you're presenting to your child, you shouldn't be too hard on yourself! No one's perfect, and how you deal with your own mistakes will teach a great deal to your child about personal responsibility and manners. If you catch yourself losing it and yelling at a telephone solicitor on the phone, explain to your son that what you did wasn't appropriate, and promise to try to avoid doing the same thing again. If you have a meltdown because of a bad day and throw a book, again, take a deep breath, and explain to your son that it was the wrong thing to do. Apologize to your son when you are being a bad example and if you've done something that gives conflicting messages or makes him feel uneasy. At the same time, reassure him that no one's perfect, not you, not him, and no one is expected to be. We can only try to be as good as possible and do our best, and live up to our errors. It will take the pressure off your child to see that he's not expected to be perfect every moment of the day, and you'll provide him with the tools to make amends and set a new course when things do go wrong.

When Stronger Measures Are Called For

Sooner or later, despite your best efforts and using all the right approaches to let your son know what is expected of him, your child's behavior will require a larger response. Certain behaviors simply cannot and should not be tolerated. Disrespect toward you; hitting, kicking, or biting; breaking things or intentionally knocking things over; ignoring household rules; and other actions that disrupt the harmony of your house and are harmful to your child and/or others require you to intervene. The behavior must be stopped! In dealing with misbehavior, the age of the child dictates the best type of intervention.

For children under two, the easiest thing to do is simply to redirect the child's attention. If he's reaching for the vase, move it and hand him a ball instead. Children this age do not respond to punishments. With older children, though, a traditional time-out or withdrawal of privileges is very effective.

The Time-Out

Children ages three to twelve usually respond well to a simple time-out. If you are going to instill discipline, the purpose of the time-out is to remove the child from the place where he is causing the problem and putting him in a place that is less stimulating where he can calm down. The key words here are *less stimulating*.

If your son's room is equipped with a TV, stereo, computer, video games, and a phone, chances are that putting him there for ten minutes may not be an effective intervention. After all, he's going to a place almost as overstimulating as the place he just left. Furthermore, nothing about being in your bedroom watching TV sets the stage for him to think about his behavior and why it was unacceptable.

Instead, many parents use a laundry room, bathroom, spare bedroom, or another spot that's been properly prepared as the "time-out spot." With the very youngest of children who require supervision at all times, time-out might be on a stool or bench or a mat in a quiet area of the kitchen or wherever you are, without any access to toys, TV, and without any interaction with you! The area needs to be quiet so that it helps create the conditions he needs to think about why he is in time-out.

With any time-out room or spot, you should choose this area carefully and screen it to be sure there's nothing potential harmful or dangerous in there your child can get into. Most experts agree that time-outs should be limited to a short span, about one minute per year of age of the child. But it's also important that the timer on the time-out does not start ticking until the child calms down. If he's put in time-out for throwing a fit, and he's continuing to yell or stomp even after he's in time-out, remind him that the timer doesn't start until he's calm and quieted down. With boys, it's also a useful tactic to give him a minute or two to decide to go to time-out when ordered rather than demanding immediate compliance. Tell your son he's to go to time-out for X number of minutes, and you'll allow him two minutes to decide to cooperate, and then turn and walk away. Don't hover and constantly remind him unless it's to let him know the two minutes are nearly over. Let him calm down for a moment, think about the consequences, and decide to cooperate on his own without being forced. When the time-out is over, it's time to hug your child and tell him you love him, and reassure him that your relationship hasn't suffered any harm. The intervention cannot be linked to a withdrawal of love and affection, so while you shouldn't try to make up with your child for preventing him from hurting people, breaking things, or disregarding essential household rules by overcompensating, a quick, warm hug, and an "I love you" lets him know he has nothing to worry about and that is sufficient.

MAKING TIME-OUT WORK FOR YOU AND YOUR SON: NOTES FROM DR. HALL.

You remove a temporarily out-of-control child from an over-stimulating environment in order to help him regain control. When helping your child regain self-control, you say words like "You are really upset right now. You need to go to your quiet place where you can calm down." Differing from what other experts say about time-out, we believe that time-out does not have to be painfully boring to be effective. Since the purpose of time-out is to help the child calm himself, we recommend you give the child a calming activity such as listening to soothing music, reading a book, or putting together a puzzle.

When the child is calm and ready to come out of time-out, you should help him indentify the specific behavior that necessitated time-out. "Yeah," he will probably admit, "I was throwing things. But it was because I was mad!" You are not interested in the why. Every child has a reason for his unacceptable behavior. What he needs to understand is that under no condition is throwing things acceptable in your house. "So it was necessary to get you away from things that could be thrown and help you calm down," you remind him.

To then instill discipline, you can take this intervention to the next level. Using questions, you can help the child figure out what he could have done instead of throwing things. In other words, you can help him learn how to control his anger. When you have helped your son develop a plan for controlling his anger, engage him in a number of role-playing activities in which he pretends to get angry and then carries out his plan to calm himself.

Now, that is instilling discipline! Sure, it takes longer than simply doling out punishment. But it is time well spent!

Some moms have said with a note of despair in their voices that their children won't cooperate with time-outs, either outright refusing to go or putting up such a fight it becomes a physical struggle, something that it is wise to avoid. If your son simply will not cooperate with time-outs, or if the misbehavior is extreme, it's time to move on to something stronger.

When Time-Outs Are Not Enough

When faced with the need to move beyond the time-out, most parents agree the most effective tactic to use is the removal of a privilege. For example, if you tell your son to head to time-out and he refuses or ignores you, the next move has to be to take away the privilege that is associated with the behavior that requires intervention. That might be his bicycle, his game system, or the right to go out to visit friends. Remove the toy or privilege for a set, stated period. Some parents combine the removal with an insistence that the child complete the time-out as well. For example, locking up a bike or skateboard for a day, beginning with the time the time-out has been completed. No time-out, no getting back the bike. Once the time-out is finished, you can start the clock ticking on getting back the privilege or toy. Other parents use an either/or tactic, so the child realizes he can either cooperate and go to a brief time-out, or be uncooperative and risk far greater consequence. You need to determine which tactic works best for your family, and then be consistent. Once again, once a time-out is over, it's time for a hug and reassurance. A child can never hear too many "I love yous," especially when he's feeling low.

No matter what the tactic you're taking, interventions should never be given in front of others. Your son should never be humiliated. If he has friends over, then quietly and politely send the others home before discussing the need for the intervention. If there's other family around, talk to your son alone in another room. Cultivate an atmosphere of respect by being respectful, even under difficult circumstances. Again, you're modeling how your son should act, so set the best example!

REMOVING PRIVILEGES TO TEACH RESPONSIBILITY: NOTES FROM DR. HALL

The privilege removed needs to be related to the problem that your son is causing. For example, what if your son gets on his bike and leaves the neighborhood without your permission? The privilege that was at the root of his disappearance is his bike. Inform him that the bicycle will be put away until he consistently demonstrates his ability to ask permission before leaving the yard. You and he can later sit down to work out what he needs to do to demonstrate that he can remember to get permission before leaving the yard. When he has demonstrated this skill, he can regain the privilege of riding his bicycle.

Working with Teens

Teens simply cannot be sent to a time-out. It would be the ultimate humiliation and treating them like a child. Instead, teen misbehavior should be dealt with by the removal of more adult privileges, such as taking away car keys, cell phones, or going to the mall. As we'll be discussing in the next section, teens should also be involved in setting up a contract for behavior, where you and your teen son can sit down and talk about what you expect of him, such as keeping curfew, using polite and acceptable language, telling the truth, being respectful of property, and acting responsibly both inside the house and out. The contract should stipulate what behavior is desired, and what measures will be taken if your son doesn't live up to his end of the bargain.

The contract idea is accepted very well by older kids, and even young adults.

THE TEACHING POWER OF NATURAL CONSEQUENCES: NOTES FROM DR. HALL

Natural consequence means what happens in the real world when a person makes a poor decision. In the story from Chapter 1, Gina's son Aric went along with his friends to pull a hay wagon down a busy public road. The natural consequence was that police intervened. Teenage boys are active, and they are hormone-driven. In that state, they often act before thinking, or at least thinking enough. When they do, boys learn best through experiencing the natural consequence of their actions. Aric certainly experienced the natural consequence of his actions. It was a lesson he was unlikely to forget, and he learned that lesson far better than he would have had his mother jumped all over him, trying to change his future behavior by making him feel stupid and guilty.

However, boys sometimes have a difficult time seeing that their actions led directly and inevitably to the natural consequence that hit them square in the face. When this happens, they need to be guided into understanding that what they did resulted in what they got. This is best done not by telling, but by asking questions and occasionally restating what had been learned.

Consider the following scenario:

The telephone rang at 2:30 in the afternoon. It was the school principal. "Jason is suspended from school tomorrow. Today, he tipped over his desk, and then threw a book at his teacher, hitting her in the face. When can you come in so that we can conference about this incident and decide what needs to be done to prevent it from happening again?"

Any mother would be livid to get that phone call, not to mention embarrassed. Your first impulse is to vent your anger by sitting your child down as soon as he crosses the threshold of the front door and giving him the what for. Then you are tempted to cap off that lecture by sending him to his room for the rest of the evening. Don't. Your son already experienced the natural consequence of his actions. When he walks through the door, his head will be down and feet will be dragging. He doesn't need further punishment. He needs help seeing what led up to him displaying behavior that resulted in being suspended from school. Accordingly, mom said, "Jason, the principal phoned. He told me that you are suspended from school tomorrow. Before supper, we need to find time to talk about what happened in school today and figure out why it happened. What time will work for you?"

"Any time, I suppose," he answers.

"Good. Let's do it now. So tell me, what was happening right before you tipped over your desk?" Mom asks.

"I couldn't find a pencil in my desk to do my math with and the teacher said right in front of the whole class, 'Jason, we are waiting for you. Get out a pencil and I will explain to everyone how to do these problems.' So I hunted and hunted in my desk for a pencil and couldn't find one and the whole class was waiting and then Derek laughed at me, calling me a retard," Jason explained.

"And then what happened?"

"I told Derek to shut up. And he didn't. He said, "What's the matter, retard? Don't ya know where ya put your pencil?" I jumped out of my desk to shut Derek's big mouth and the top of it was open. I didn't mean to push it over, it just went over and everything spilled on the floor. Derek laughed at me. I didn't throw the book at the teacher. I threw it at Derek, but he ducked and it accidentally hit the teacher."

"Jason," mom replies, "let me tell you what I heard and you tell me if I have it right. I heard that this all started because you couldn't find a pencil. The teacher waited to give her instructions until you found a pencil, but look as hard as you could, you couldn't find one. Then Derek called you a retard, and you got angry at Derek, so angry that you accidentally tipped over your desk, and then you threw a book at him. Is that right?"

"Yeah."

"So what started the whole thing?" Mom asks.

"What do you mean?" Jason asked.

"If you had a pencil when the teacher asked you to get your pencil, would you have tipped over your desk and hit the teacher with a book?"

"Nope."

"So, what would have been the best thing to do when you couldn't find your pencil?" Mom asked.

"I looked and looked everything for my pencil. Honest I did," Jason replied.

"Yes. You looked and you looked your hardest. But when you didn't find your pencil, what could you have done?"

"I don't know," Jason said, looking confused.

"Brenda sits right behind you. Do you think Brenda had an extra pencil?"

"Probably."

"Does that give you an idea?" Mom asked.

"Do you mean I could have asked Brenda for a pencil?"

"If you had asked Brenda for a pencil, would you have tipped over your desk and hit the teacher with a book?"

"I get it," Jason said, nodding his head as he reflected on how simple it would have been to avoid the whole disaster.

The Point System

Parenting expert Corrie Lynne Player, author of *Loving Firmness: Successfully Raising Teenagers Without Losing Your Mind* and *The Everything® Parent's Guide to Raising an Adopted Child*, developed a useful system of rewards that she refers to as an anger-free discipline system, based on her experiences as a foster parent for over forty troubled kids, in addition to raising her own nine children! Explains Player, "the Point System's been developed over the course of twenty years, and it was originally developed with our special needs foster home for challenged teenagers who needed serious intervention to change some toxic behaviors." While many institutions have long utilized a reward/punishment system, Player adapted the concept for family use, and it's flexible enough to suit any family's needs and practices. In fact, Player admits with a laugh, "About fifteen years ago I realized my foster kids were a whole lot better behaved and had a better attitude than my own children!"

With the Point System, parents grade children on three basic categories: attitude, maintaining their personal space, and chores, using a scale of one-to-ten. The child's progress is recorded in a book or on a chart. Points earned are linked to privileges and special treats. So if a child wants to play a video game, he has to have enough points earned. Chores could be linked to allowance, so if the child wishes to receive his allowance, he has to have completed enough of the chores. A child can also earn extra points for doing something nice, like sharing with a sibling without being asked, or giving his seat on a bus to an elderly person or a pregnant woman.

With younger kids, mom should be the one to determine what goals and behaviors they're looking for, and what behaviors should earn or lose points, and how many. In the case of teenagers, though, standards and expectations, as well as what's required to earn various privileges or treats, should be discussed at a family conference. With older children, the more you bring them into the process, the more cooperative they'll be, since they've been a part of creating the system!

The key must be that the privilege or treat is linked to the behavior, and without good behavior, there is no reward. Consistency is absolutely essential!

A New Attitude!

Under the category of attitude, a mom might grade such things as how politely the child answered a question or how cooperative the kid was at homework time. Doing a chore, but doing it with a snarl and a grimace, cannot be treated the same as doing the chore with a smile and a positive attitude. So the child may earn his points for doing a chore, but may also lose some points in the attitude column if he was surly or negative.

When starting the Point System, it's best to focus most strongly on the behaviors the parent is most looking to correct or reinforce. "In the beginning, the mom can allow the child a chance to earn back points lost as they learn what's expected of them," Player suggests. So, if your son slammed a door angrily after speaking with you, you'd deduct points, but if he then was able to calm down and come back to you and explain calmly that he realized it was wrong and apologize, you could remove the negative mark. But later on, as the child becomes more aware of the standards you expect and what the consequences of actions are, you need to become stricter, and you have to be very firm about sticking to your set rules for earning privileges. Rewards have to be linked to the behavior and the points, or you're just exercising your accounting skills and teaching the child he can either pout or negotiate his way around the rules. "That's the most important part of the Point System," Player stresses, "that it's tied to 'wants' the kid might have. Whatever they want, they should not be able to get it unless they have the right number of points, whether it's dessert, watching videos with friends, or going to the school's football game on Friday night."

In addition, "The emphasis has to be on giving them rewards for a good attitude, not on disciplining for a poor one," explains Player. "So if they exhibit a bad attitude, you quietly make a note of it on the chart and deduct the points, and don't make a big deal of it. But if they do something positive and show a good attitude, then it's time to really go wild and say 'Wow, you did a great job and you've earned ten points!'" Each family personalizes the system so it addresses the situations it's dealing with.

With the youngest kids, Player uses a variation she calls the Chocolate Chip Point System where the mom uses objects in a jar (could be chips, or beads, or ping pong balls, whatever works for you!). Over the course of the day, you can put them in and take them out as the child's behavior warrants, and at the end of the day, add them up to see how many the child has earned. Some users of the Point System use a bankbook system and keep track of points in an account, making deposits; when the child wants something like a special treat, he has to have enough points in his account.

Maintaining Personal Space

As mentioned, the second category monitored in the Point System is maintaining the teen's personal spaces. This includes picking up after himself and keeping his room clean. "Teenagers," Player reminds us, "are really great at just walking in the house and tossing a coat on the chair and making a snack and demolishing the kitchen!" Again, using a scale of one-to-ten, the mom tracks how well the child is maintaining the space and uses the criteria established jointly with the child at the family meeting. So perhaps you both agree that it isn't necessary that the bed be made every day as long as the sheets get changed regularly, but you insist that dirty laundry be tossed in the hamper and not on the floor. If the teen makes a snack, you might expect him to clean the counters free of crumbs and put his dishes in the sink, but you might not insist he wash them right away. You have to set the standards based on the goals you're looking to achieve for your family and your home. The important thing is that you maintain the standards you've agreed to set.

When you first start monitoring this for the chart, you'll need to evaluate several times a day, such as before leaving for school, before dinner, and before bedtime, but later on, you can reduce it to just one check a day before bed.

Chores Are Vital

The final aspect the Point System tracks is the child's chores. "Giving a kid responsibilities is what gives the kid's personality a chance to develop," Player says. While chores seem to have fallen out of favor in many families in recent years—and quite a few of the families I've encountered don't give their sons regular family responsibilities at all, or assign household duties only to the daughters—recent studies have confirmed the value of giving regular tasks to children. While at times it might seem quicker and less trouble to just do something yourself, it's worth the extra effort to teach kids to handle household tasks. A study by Marty

Rosssman of the University of Minnesota followed a group of kids from early childhood through to early adulthood and found that those kids who'd been given chores to do were more successful as adults than those who hadn't had chores. They were more likely to stay in school, had more successful careers, and weren't as likely to use drugs. This study specifically noted that children should start doing chores early in their lives, as young as three or four years of age, since those who only started being given tasks as teens actually fared worse, though other factors could have also been responsible for that effect, such as a changed family circumstance that otherwise disrupted the teen's life. The early assignment of family responsibilities seemed to bolster the child's confidence and assurance, since Mom was trusting him to take care of something. It also set the tone for a lifelong self-reliance and linking of hard work and delayed gratification with the achievement of goals and the fulfillment of wishes and desires. As part of the Point System, the child is given a small stroke at the time the chore is finished ("Great job! You remembered to take out the trash and that means ten points!), as well as the larger reward of the privilege or allowance money at the end of the week or the month when the points are tallied.

Kids should be given a to-do list with their assigned chores clearly printed on it, and a chance to check each item off as they complete it. That way, you won't have to chase after them reminding them what they're supposed to do or listen to arguments about whether or not anyone ever told them what to do. When assigning a task for the first time, be sure to carefully go over how to do the job and what's expected. Kids can be pretty creative in interpreting what "clean" means. I was really delighted to see how quickly my youngest son, Aric, took care of changing the litter in our rabbits' cages until I realized he was simply pouring more cedar shavings on top of the old ones! I didn't catch on until the rabbit barely had head clearance in the hutch! However, once we went over the process and discussed why it was important for the rabbit's health to have a clean, dry environment, we didn't have any more problems (with that!). So, if you assign the child to do his own laundry, take time to explain when to use hot water and when to use cold, and why the red T-shirt shouldn't be in with the white underwear.

By giving boys responsibilities, you'll be teaching them self-sufficiency, helping them gain self-esteem, and taking some of the pressure off of yourself! Becoming disciplined, in attitude and behavior, will benefit your child and prepare him for a successful adult life.

As a Mom of a Remarkable Boy, you

- Are strong enough to be a parent rather than just a pal;
- Don't confuse discipline with punishment;
- Understand that the way a directive is presented is key, and use the proper tone and wording;
- Link rewards and privileges to desired behavior;
- Know consistency is vital;
- Set a good example, but understand no one is perfect;
- Give your son a few minutes to decide to cooperate rather than expecting immediate compliance;
- Never uses an intervention to humiliate; and
- Reassure your son that your love is constant and not conditional.

CHAPTER 10

Communication Is Key

Communication with your son begins at birth, and often our mode and method of communication with our sons early in their lives will dictate the path of our relationships with them later in life.

More Than Just Words

Beyond speech, we're communicating far more than words and language skills when we interact with our young sons, and communicating is far from limited to the words we speak. We communicate with our sons, and with everyone else around us, using complex signals of body language, eye contact, and even the pitch, volume, and cadence of our voice.

"The strongest protective device for a child in adolescence," Karyn Purvis, Director of the Texas Christian University's Institute of Child Development and co-author of *The Connected Child*, explains, "is first a strong sense of who he is that comes through nurturing as an infant; looking into his eyes, touching, and that strong sense of connection to us that says 'I know who you are, and I know your preciousness.'" That sense of "preciousness," as Dr. Purvis has termed it, is the strong, deep sense of value and worth that allows a child to know he's special, he's important, and he's loved, and we as mothers can instill that sense of "preciousness" in our sons through our communication with them. By looking into his eyes, touching him, and cuddling him, you're letting your child know his importance, and this will help him later in life. That deep understanding that he is loved and valued is vital to your son's development.

BONDING: NOTES FROM DR. HALL

This mother-infant communication is the basis of the critically important bond that needs to form, for this mother-infant bond is foundation and blueprint that the child will use for all his future relationships. In order for a strong mother-infant bond to develop, the mother must accurately read and then consistently respond in a nurturing way to the child's cues (his language, so to speak). When he is hungry, she must hear that in his fussing. When his diaper is wet, she must hear that in his vocalizations and movements. When he is content and wants to be held and cuddled, she must also hear that and respond accordingly.

Psychologists also describe a phenomenon called "matching," in which a mother and baby mimic each other's sounds, movements, eyes contact, even sleep cycles! Matching, along with the strong nurturing attention and care giving, helps bond mother and child and build secure attachments. You can help aid in this by consciously matching your child's actions, and by communicating with him at eye level by sitting on the floor with him. This sends the unspoken message that you're really listening and being responsive to your child. Children must gain a sense of trust that they'll be heard when they speak to you. In that way, Dr. Purvis says, the child is given his voice. "Matching" reinforces his sense of self-worth and protects him from the negative forces he'll encounter later in life, like drug use and untrustworthy adults.

Another important element to making sure your child knows he is being heard is to really give him your full attention. Turn away from whatever else you're doing, like watching TV, or doing the dishes, and turn your face and body toward him when he speaks to you. That way, he knows he has your full attention, that you're really listening, and that you feel what he has to say is important.

SELF-CONTROL: NOTES FROM DR. HALL

Your early communication with your son also forms the basis by which he acquires the ability for self-control. Initially, a toddler's language is connected to his actions and his interactions with an adult, usually his mother. The mother's language directs the child's actions. For example, the mother might say, "Where is your bottle?" In response, the child looks for his bottle. The mother's language directed his actions. Mother's ability to use language to direct the child's action depends, of course, on her using language intentionally and for a meaningful purpose. If the mother were to frequently, teasingly say things like "Where is your bottle?" and there were no bottle, the child would soon stop looking for his bottle, and, more subtly, stop attending to his mother's language.

However, in the normal course of mother-infant interactions, the child comes to internalize his mother's language to direct his own behavior. In other words, he starts to use words that his mother had used to direct his own behavior. You have no doubt observed this. A child walking up to a hot pan that just came out of the oven, suddenly says, "Hot. Don't touch." Having said that, the child quickly retracts his hand and avoids getting burnt. When he is only a year or so older, he no longer talks to himself, but his internal language still says, "Hot. Don't touch." He is now using internal language to direct his actions. At this point, psychologists and linguists say that the child has "behavior-regulating thought," which you and I call self-control.

It's Also How We Say It

What are you communicating to your son with your voice and your tone? Are you giving him confidence, and projecting that he's safe with you because you're in control and able to protect him? Or is the very way you're speaking conveying to your son that you're overwhelmed and out of control?

Dr. Purvis relates the way we speak to the vocalizations of animals. A high-pitched, rapid sounding from an animal relays panic and fear to the other animals around it. It tells those other animals, "I'm not safe, and neither are you!" If you're addressing your son in a voice that's relaying that you're overwhelmed, your child will not feel safe to trust you to protect and take care of him. And that's where behavior problems can begin to arise.

It's natural to speak to a very young infant in a soft, high-pitched rapid voice. They giggle and squeal their delight and vocalize back. But once your child becomes a toddler, it's time to moderate your voice to project, calm, control, and reassurance. Males, in particular, respond better to a slightly lower pitch and somewhat louder volume. Speak clearly and directly. If you're attempting to redirect your son when he's misbehaving, and you find the pitch of your voice rising to a sound that's only audible to dogs, it's time to become more aware of how you're speaking. Dr. Purvis recommends videotaping or audiotaping your interactions with your child to see how you're conveying your message to your son. "It's all in the TVC," she explains. "It's all about Total Voice Control in tone, volume, and cadence." If you need to redirect your child or make certain you're being heard, you should take a deep breath, stand with your legs slightly apart in a power stance, and speak to your son in a low, louder, slower voice (your power voice). Not yelling, just projecting more than you would in quiet conversation. That voice conveys confidence and assurance, and it also assures them you're the boss. This voice works just as well for school-age children and teens. In fact, I've found it most effective with teens, and to this day, though my children are all grown now, others around me can tell when I'm speaking to one of my sons on the phone because they hear me using the boy voice.

You should also be aware of allowing your voice to rise in pitch around your child when dealing with household situations. Even if you're not speaking directly to your child, he can sense your anxiety and picks up on it. Always project calm, confidence, and control. Let your child know in the way you speak that you have the situation under control and that he's protected and taken care of, and you'll lessen his anxiety.

"With my kids and my mother who lived with us, we had a lot of medical emergencies in our house. One of my sons had seizures, and my mom had serious heart problems. At first, these things were really frightening for the children to witness, but I realized that I could really influence their reactions with my own. I forced myself to keep my voice calm and low-pitched. Soon the kids weren't terrified by what was going on, but calmly pitching in to see what they could do to help, and I found them copying the way I spoke when they would address each other in a crisis. I know if I'd projected panic, my kids would have suffered a lot of anxiety."

—*Anne, mother of two sons and one daughter*

The high-pitched squeaky voice coming from your toddler also conveys messages. Everyone's heard that high-pitched scream that toddlers make (the one that sets your nerves, and teeth, on edge). Humans and other animals are hard-wired to be unable to ignore that sound. It's guaranteed to bring attention. However, what your child is conveying with that sound is that they're not getting *enough* of your attention, and they have to resort to that sound to bring you around. They're insecure in your attention, and they don't trust you to meet their needs. If you find your toddler-age son squealing in a pitch designed to shatter glass, try some reassuring, nurturing exchanges. It's difficult for a single mom who has so very many responsibilities to be able to always stop what she's doing to give attention to her child, but keep in mind that there's nothing more important you could possibly be doing than being with your child. The interaction you have now will be setting the groundwork for his future relationships with you, and with the rest of the world.

Helping with Your Son's Verbal Skills

Sooner or later, you're going to realize that your son has a style of communication that is distinctly male. "Little girls are more skilled in words," says Karyn Purvis, "but little boys are stronger in nonverbal communication. The girls will often start out making verbal sounds, word sounds, but little boys often start out making noises like truck noises, airplane noises, and bulldozer sounds." But what causes boys' verbal skills to lag behind girls? Beyond the differences in brain development mentioned earlier in the book, studies have determined that parents often spend less time talking with their infant sons than with their infant daughters, a fact some researchers point to explain why young boys' verbal development lags behind girls and to explain those brain differences. Some experts believe parents spend less time talking to their baby boys because baby boys respond less to faces and make less eye

contact, so the baby himself seems less connected, and others feel
that parents simply cuddle and coo less to boys because they feel
boys should be "tougher" than girls. Yet many parents, particularly moms, disagree vehemently and feel they spend just as much
time interacting and speaking to their boys as they do with their
daughters. Regardless of your own view, the benefits of continual
communication with your child are irrefutable.

> "It's much harder to talk at home with the competition
> of toys, computer, music, and TV. One day a couple of
> years ago, we were on a walk, and Sam asked a ques-
> tion about something (I don't remember what). The dis-
> cussion turned into a whole discussion of racism and its
> impact on the school system. A casual question from my
> son, and we have a fifteen or twenty minute conversation
> about race in society. As I said, he's a talker, very smart,
> very empathetic, very intuitive."
>
> —Jamio, mother of one

Family therapist Steve Biddulph suggests parents can improve
their child's verbal abilities by "talking up"—that is, by speaking
back to them a stage ahead of the child's own verbal phase. So
if the child is a toddler speaking one word, for instance, "ball,"
reply to him in two or three words, like "big ball," or "big, red
ball." If your child is speaking phrases, reply to him in complete
sentences. Continually present a more sophisticated level of
speaking for your son to learn and mimic. By challenging your
son's verbal abilities and constantly teaching new ones, you'll give
your son a much needed boost to his language skills. Biddulph
also emphasizes the kind of constant explanation of what is going
on around the child and how things work, as I described in my
section on make home a learning laboratory in Chapter 3. This
easy, steady influx of knowledge, new vocabulary, and new ideas

gives you son an excellent learning platform for his later schoolwork. Finally, Biddulph stresses reading out loud to your child as often as possible, and creating games of familiar stories. If your child knows how a story goes from previous readings, make him "fill in the blanks," or suggest changes or add silly new endings. This will keep him alert and his mind engaged.

How Your Son Talks

As a female, you may be accustomed to a very intimate style of communication. The idea of the heart-to-heart dialogue, where you take your son by the hand and sit him down and gaze into his eyes while asking him about his feelings or what's going on in his life probably seems like the best way of keeping in touch and getting to the bottom of things. But you're probably also finding yourself a bit frustrated by your son's responses.

> "I do think there are differences (between boys and girls), reluctantly. My son and I talk best when we're doing something else, like walking to school. I back off and acknowledge that it's hard to talk about feelings or personal things, leave him space and time, but am always clear that things won't just be forgotten. He's quite good at having it worked out by the time I raise the subject again."
>
> —*Emily, single mom*

Unlike girls, boys tend to need space to communicate their feelings and may sometimes need to go off and be left alone for a while to process their thoughts and then come back to the topic later. Talking while doing activities, like riding in a car, doing chores side by side like the dishes, or playing games, often allows your son the comfort zone he needs to get around to talking about personal subjects. He also needs to move at his own pace.

Pushing too hard, too fast, will cause him to shut down, and you're likely to get responses like "fine," "nothing," or "whatever." Child psychologists often recommend combining dialogue with action. As I'd mentioned in the introduction to this book, my own sons were extremely uncommunicative until I discovered their secret trigger, riding in the car. For other children, playing a board game or tossing or kicking a ball around might help. Play a game, ride bikes, walk the dog, or do some other joint activity until your son feels relaxed and let him guide the conversation. Even with the buffer of an activity in the mix, this is still no time to interrogate. Push too hard, and he's certain to shut down.

Boys Will Be Boys: The "Strong, Silent Type"

Mothers sometimes mistakenly think that boys don't think as much about emotions, or don't have the same need to communicate, but quite the opposite, they need more of our help learning how and being encouraged to talk about their feelings. Simply because they don't do it now doesn't mean they don't need to, or that they wouldn't be happier and more secure boys if they learned to talk about their emotions.

Some of the moms I communicated with felt it was simply the nature of boys to become silent and less communicative, particularly as they grow into teens. Regrettably, it's too easy to accept the decline in communication. But it's truly not in the child's best interests. Even if it takes work and time, strive to keep the communication flowing. Show your son that he can be safe communicating his feelings to you, and that you will respect and accept them.

How do we build the trust boys need to feel safe communicating? One vital component is that we listen without judging. In fact, just listen. If we express discomfort, shock, or disapproval, or try to negate our son's emotions ("Oh, come now, you can't really feel that way!"), we're teaching him to hide those emotions from us. Much of what a boy will voice when he feels safe to talk may feel foreign to women, and it may be difficult for us to accept or understand. But by trying to convince your boy his feelings are inappropriate or incorrect, by trying to convince him that only the female reaction or impression is correct, we'll force him back underground. Instead, listen with an open mind and an accepting heart. Be accessible, be eager to listen to what he has to say, and help him explore his feelings.

> "I think that girls communicate differently from boys—but at this point, I feel that my son is fairly communicative about emotions. He knows, and has known for quite some time, how to tell me that he is sad, scared, shy, and so on. I won't forget the day he told me was not shy anymore. When I asked him why he wasn't shy anymore, he said, 'Because I am so happy!'"
>
> —*Tamar, single mom*

Boys, more than girls, need to learn how to communicate their feelings. They also need to be assured that feeling those emotions and talking about them doesn't make the boy weak. Typical "boy" society teaches boys to hide their vulnerability, since being vulnerable makes the boy appear weak. This limits the emotions he might feel comfortable expressing. If a boy is told that showing pain, sadness, or loneliness makes him less masculine or that "only girls cry," or is ridiculed as "gay" for expressing tenderness or compassion, boys not only learn that those emotions are unacceptable but also develop an ingrained notion of the inferiority of girls and a sense of homophobia. Be constantly alert to these corrosive messages, and correct them where you encounter them. If your son's uncle if trying to teach your son to pitch and chides him for "throwing like a girl," explain why you don't want those messages presented to your son. If you hear your son using homophobic epithets to tease friends, immediately make your son aware that that is unacceptable and explain why it's dangerous and damaging.

How to Teach Your Son to Talk about His Feelings

Researchers have theorized that boys may have a difficult time speaking about their bad feelings because the parts of their brain that controls language, the cerebral cortex, isn't that well connected to the area of the brain where negative emotions are processed, in the amygdala. Females (and yes, that includes us, Mom!), on the other hand, soon begin to process their emotions and discuss them more clearly because the "seat" of their emotions moves during adolescence to the cerebral cortex, the language center. But expecting to put a direct question to a boy about how he feels is guaranteed to make a boy squirm with discomfort.

Instead, you can help your child identify and communicate his feelings appropriately. Give him the words to communicate his feelings by teaching him to communicate emotions like sadness, jealousy, embarrassment, loneliness, fear, emotional hurt, and grief. One way to do this is to make a game of it (the indirect approach works so well with boys!). Take turns making faces and expressions that signify different emotions and have the other one try to guess what you're acting out. Once they guess correctly, you should each tell the other a story about a time you experienced that emotion. Start with basic, easy emotions, like *afraid*, *happy*, or *sad*, and work toward more complex feelings like *lonely*, *jealous*, and *hurt*.

Even after we've given our sons the words and safety to express their feelings, we need to be aware of the male need to take his own time to open up. I learned (several times over!) that a boy cannot be rushed into communication and opening up (even though as moms we're anxious to know what's bothering them). A boy will often withdraw and gather his thoughts before attempting to discuss them with you. Often, he just needs to figure out exactly what it is that he is feeling. The best we can do as mothers is be patient and keep alert to the signs he might be ready to talk.

A boy under stress will withdraw and become uncommunicative. Unlike females, who often call all their best girlfriends to come bring comfort and something chocolate when things go wrong, boys go off by themselves. And mothers, being who we are, try to follow and talk out the problem, which turns out to only make the situation worse!

In Peggy Drexler's study of single moms, she found that some of the moms found it beneficial to give their sons some time and space after a blowup. So, instead of immediately following after your son after an outburst or volatile exchange, demanding to find out what's going on, it may be more productive to back off and let him have some time to work things out, calm down, and then come back later on. In my own experience (and having had several teens under the roof all at one time, emotions seemed to run high), I felt the boys were embarrassed by their own outbursts and needed to regain a little control before they wanted me to see them again, so they could save face. In early puberty, your son is likely to misread your cues and respond more emotionally and irrationally, and sometimes a little time to chill and think things through is really what's needed most. It's probably completely against the nature of many women to not try to talk it out right away, but it's not really typical of male communication.

By realizing that, as women talking to males, we have a great deal to learn about the way males communicate, by respecting both the mode and the timing males need to feel safe to open up, and by giving our sons the words and the freedom to express themselves without fear, we can help our sons grow into expressive, sensitive men, and avoid the trap of the "strong, silent type."

Sometimes, a book can help a child understand and communicate his feelings, and talking about a story can help you discuss some of the issues your son may be dealing with. Here are some suggestions for books to share with your child:

- *All My Feelings at Preschool: Nathan's Day* (*Let's Talk about Feelings*), by Susan Conlin. For ages four to eight. Parenting Press (1990). A boy expresses a range of emotions during his day, including feelings of rejection and sadness.
- *Was It the Chocolate Pudding? A Story for Little Kids about Divorce,* by Sandra Levins, Bryan Langdo (Illustrator). For age two to six. American Psychological Association (2005). Deals with the various issues that arise in a divorce, like single-parent homes and joint custody, and reassures it's not the child's fault.
- *Mom and Dad Break Up.* Joan Singleton Prestine, Virginia Klyberg (Illustrator). For ages four to eight. School Specialty Press (2001). A young boy talks about his feelings when his parents break up, and how he now sees them separately. Reassuring.
- *Two Homes.* Claire Masurel, Kady MacDonald Denton (Illustrator). For ages two to five. Candlewick (2001). A wonderfully reassuring book featuring Alex, a young son of a divorced couple, who compares his experiences at Mommy's house and at Daddy's, while always knowing he is well loved by both parents.
- *As the Crow Flies.* Elizabeth Winthrop, Joan Sandin (Illustrator). For ages four to eight. Clarion (1998). A young boy with divorced parents misses his father when he's with his mom, and misses his mom when he's with his dad. He finally confronts his father and gains a greater understanding. Depicts a very close and loving relationship with a long-distance dad.
- *On the Day His Daddy Left,* by Eric J. Adams, Kathleen Adams, Layne Johnson (Illustrator). For ages four to eight. Albert Whitman reprint edition (2003). On the day his father moves out of the house, a child talks to the many people around him, who all assure him that his parent's divorce is not his fault.

161

- *My Mom and Dad Don't Live Together Anymore: A Drawing Book for Children of Separated or Divorced Parents.* By Judith Aron Rubin, Bonnie Matthews (Illustrator). For ages four to eight. Magination Press (2002). Helps kids cope and express themselves through pictures and words.
- *Something's Different,* by Shelley Rotner, Sheila M. Kelly. For ages four to eight. Millbrook Press (2002). Explains a young child's emotions as he copes with his parents' marital problems.
- *A Solitary Blue,* by Cynthia Voigt. For teens, Aladdin (2003). Deals with parental abandonment (in this one, by the mother) and return, and the mending of relationships with both parents. A very sensitive story about the pain parents can inflict on children, and about children's longing for closeness.
- *Holly Starcross,* by Berlie Doherty. For ages nine to twelve. HarperCollins Children's (2002). A fourteen-year-old girl meets her father for the first time in eight years, which deeply impacts her view of her father, her mother, and herself.

As a Mom of a Remarkable Boy, you

- Communicate love and reassurance to you son with your eyes, your words, and your gestures;
- Know that boys might need help learning to name and communicate their feelings;
- Make certain you hear your son in order to give him his voice;
- Use a strong, firm, and confident voice when communicating with your son;
- Give your son the space he needs to be comfortable talking, but are always an eager listener; and
- Use activities, games, and car rides as "talk starters," rather than looking for face-to-face confrontations.

CHAPTER 11

Academics

From ages five through eighteen, a boy will spend most of his waking hours engaging in school activities, either in the classroom or at home. His social world also becomes largely his classmates, and he may spend more time under the guidance of his teacher each day than he does interacting directly with you, his mother. It's easy to see how the school experience can have a tremendous influence on your son's outlook, his perception of himself, and his hopes for the future.

School and Your Son

The other adults interacting with your child for six or seven hours a day, and the quality of that interaction, is key to how your son views school. Is he made to feel self-confident, self-assured, and comfortable? Is his classroom "boy-friendly," and do the subjects interest and engage him? Or does he feel stifled, humiliated, bored, and misunderstood?

What's expected of children today is far different from expectations of even just twenty years ago. When I (and many of you) attended school in the 1960s and 1970s, kindergarten was a half-day filled with play, music, painting, fanciful stories, and naptime. Today, kindergarten children are expected to arrive prepared for the first day of class knowing their letters, numbers, and colors, and are often expected to have some rudimentary reading skills. Liability issues have caused many schools to forbid children from arriving more than a few minutes before class begins, which precludes a quick game of baseball or footraces before the bell rings. Instead, children are rising from bed, riding to school in a bus or a car, and then tromping inside to sit down directly at their seats, never having any chance to expend any of that energy that's built up over a night of being still and resting! Free play is extremely limited, particularly for a young child who needs a great deal of creative and unrestricted exuberant play, and a five-year-old is expected to sit quietly at a table or desk for nearly a full day. The pace and volume of learning has accelerated at a phenomenal pace, and the highly literature-based content and style of teaching, which is not necessarily the most conducive for learning for young boys, is leaving our sons behind. Sons of single mothers, especially, seem to be at a disadvantage. But what's really at work behind the statistics?

School and the Fatherless Boy

As discussed at the beginning of this book, boys raised in homes without mothers seem to have more difficulties than do children from two-parent homes. They drop out more, engage in more disruptive behavior, and get poorer grades. But is the absence of a father the real root cause? A study by Henry Ricciuti of Cornell University, published in the September 1999 issue of the *Journal of Family Psychology*, explored just that question. Ricciuti followed a group of grade-school boys and studied their lives and their home demographics at two separate periods of their lives. His conclusion was that, "Our findings suggest that when maternal and household characteristics are favorable, single parenthood, in and of itself, is not necessarily a risk factor for children's school readiness." In another study by the RAND Institution on Education and Training, "Student Achievement and the Changing American Family," researchers examined family characteristics and student performance and managed to separate out income, parental education, working mothers, and single parenthood, and the conclusion was that the single most important factor for a child's educational success was the education of the parent. The more education the parent attained, the better the child performed in school. Other factors, like the mother's marital status or job situation, weighed in as minor considerations.

The Academic Pressures on Boys

One of the moms I interviewed, Rachel, summed up a very common experience for moms of early school-age boys, particularly now with the increased performance demands placed on schools and the increasing reliance on a literature-based curriculum. She told me, "I was stunned to get a note home early on in my son's first grade year telling me that he was reading below grade level. He was a strong reader and loved books, and often sat on my bed reading to me from books I recall reading in third grade! He was placed in a 'special group' and the parents of the 'special' kids were all invited to come to a meeting to discuss the children's needs. You could probably guess that nearly all the 'special' kids were boys! The principal and a reading specialist explained to us that the new No Child Left Behind rules had really put pressure on the schools to increase the pace, and our school system, in particular, had elevated their standards above even the state standards. They even apologized, stating that they realized that the standards were really hard to achieve. Later on, after I became familiar with the designations for the various reading levels, I was able to determine that my "slow reader" son was reading all of two weeks behind the class goal! He's one of the youngest kids in the class, having stated kindergarten at four, so some kids in his class are nearly a year older than him, which means a lot when they're so young. The pressure and expectations on the kids is incredible." In a quick follow-up to this interview, Rachel informed me that by the end of the school year, her son was now reading on grade level and meeting all grade level expectations.

Learning "Boy-Style"

Does your son's school provide an environment that's stimulating for your son? Are there boy-friendly subjects? Does English or reading class include books and stories that would interest a male reader? Is he allowed to write about things that interest him and in ways that appeal to him?

Since most teachers are women, they naturally gravitate to materials that appeal and seem interesting to them but that may leave their males students less than entranced. Talk to your son about his class work. What interests and excites him the most? Was there a project he particularly enjoyed, and why did it interest him? What types of work appeal to him the least? Work together with your son's teacher to find ways to fully engage your child in his school subjects. If the teacher assigns essays to encourage writing, can your son choose a topic that particularly intrigues him? Perhaps "What I did over summer vacation" would have your son falling asleep at his desk, but "My visit to Dinosaur Park" would give him a chance to really shine. One of my grandsons refused to cooperate with writing journal reports of how he spent his weekend following his visitation weekends with his father. He had too many conflicting emotions and wasn't ready to share too much information with a relative stranger like his new teacher since they hadn't build up a bank of trust yet between them. Instead, we asked that he be allowed to write about other things going on in his life and fun adventures he'd taken with his mother until he felt ready to participate in the regular assignment. This special consideration was only necessary for about six weeks, and once he'd settled into the new schedule, had acclimated to his new home and school, and became familiar with the visitation routine, he was once again happy to participate in all the regular assignments.

Boys learn best through physical manipulation, a style unsupported in most contemporary classrooms, which emphasize rote learning and quiet reading. Boys also possess a high degree of restlessness and energy that simply isn't addressed in most classrooms. Rather than providing a boy-friendly environment that encourages males to learn in their own style and allows them to burn off excess energy (which would, in turn, allow them to sit quietly for periods), males are diagnosed as hyperactive and disruptive and prescribed Ritalin to make them conform to the teacher's expectations, which are based on ideal female behavior. Boys, says one specialist in male behavior, are being treated like defective girls.

Obviously, there can't be twenty-five different curriculums to suit twenty-five students in a class, and the work cannot be individualized to the extent that it makes it impossible to grade students' performance fairly relative to each other. But there should be enough variety to keep a range of children stimulated and to appeal to a range of interests. Parental involvement in the school and in the classroom is one of the best ways you can find out what, and how, your children are taught. Volunteer in your son's classroom, schedule regular conferences with his teacher, and meet with the teacher at the start of the new term to go over the curriculum and the teacher's expectations. Do this proactively, before any problems arise, and you'll achieve a better result for your son and have a better working relationship with the teacher for those moments when you need the teacher's support and cooperation.

In a study published by Paul Dawson in 1971 titled *Fatherless Boys, Teacher Perceptions and Male Teacher Influence*, teachers were tested as to their perceptions of fatherless boys. Teachers tended to assume that the students from fatherless homes would be more likely to have behavior issues and emotional problems, and to have academic difficulties. The natural concern is that these predeterminations could be self-fulfilling prophecies. Your early and interested participation in your son's classroom will go far to dispel any negative preconceptions your son's teacher may have.

More than girls, boys need to be interested in the subject matter in order to really excel in school. In a study reported in the *Journal of Educational Psychology*, authors Angela Lee Duckworth and Martin E. P. Seligman of the University of Pennsylvania tried to determine the reason behind the differing performances of male and female students on different kinds of tests. They determined that there's a distinct gender difference in the level of self-discipline. Girls can focus and apply a sustained effort toward a long-term goal, despite boredom or a lack of interest, while boys tended to lack that level of self-discipline. Boys started their homework later, and spent half as much time on it. Their approach was basically "get in and get it done as quickly as they could," particularly if something wasn't interesting to them. This difference in self-discipline is often the reason behind the difference in report card grades. Boys, however, still have an advantage on achievement tests and IQ tests, which require a short-term effort, and often rely heavily on the sort of multiple-choice questions that boys do best at. Finding ways to make the subject matter interesting to males, both in the classroom and at home, will help classroom performance and enhance your son's educational experience and his perception of school. You can also suggest to the teacher to seat boys closer to the front of the room. As discussed earlier in the book, boys often can't hear as well as girls, or they may be more easily distracted, and putting him closer to the action will help him engage more fully.

Things That Help Teach "Boy-Style":

- Using maps, drawings, and illustrations
- Using models or actual items the boy can touch, handle, and manipulate

- Using video in addition to literature-based learning
- Advocating for more computer-based learning

Male Teachers

In the second part of the study by Paul Dawson mentioned earlier, twenty-two fourth-grade fatherless boys were studied for an entire school year, half in male teacher classroom and half in a female teacher classroom. The male teacher classroom's boys consistently showed greater overall gains in social and emotional development over the course of the school year. The boys had significantly higher scores in terms of self-confidence, feelings of self-worth, and acceptance of responsibility. Other studies have shown similar significant advantages to having male teachers.

Encourage your son's school to seek out and recruit male teachers. The majority of teachers are female, particularly in elementary school, so schools need to make a special effort to bring in male teachers. The advantages to the students definitely balance the effort.

Fighting for the Return of Recess

The pressure on schools to teach an ever-accelerating curriculum and report an ever-increasing percentage of their students passing standardized achievement tests has created a time squeeze in the class day. The Federal government is now expecting to see all children testing proficient in science, language arts, and math by 2014. For most schools, that has meant cutting into time for recess and other free playtime. A 1999 survey of 15,000 school districts performed by the American Association for the Child's Right to Play found that 40 percent of school districts were either eliminating recess, cutting back on it, or considering one or the other. Prior to this, elementary schools often incorporated several brief recess periods into the school day. But is recess really important? Aren't children supposed to be in school to learn?

> "I'd gotten feedback from my son's teacher that he seemed distracted and restless in class, popping up and out of his desk and moving around. It was obvious he needed more activity, but the school schedule rarely allowed for him to periodically run around. So we're going to start walking to school in the morning instead of taking the bus. In the long run, I think it will be a big help in allowing him to settle down for his morning classes.
>
> —*Rachel, mother of two boys*

Many specialists feel that free play during recess is actually an important opportunity for social development and learning, and is important for the good health of the students; there's no research supporting the notion that recess is harmful or without benefit. Yet only three states require some sort of recess during the school day, and only a handful more recommend it without regulating it. Is it more than just coincidence that there's been a rise in the diagnosis of ADD (attention deficit disorder) and ADHD (attention-deficit hyperactivity disorder), most markedly among our boys, concurrently with the disappearance of recess?

In addition to limiting or eliminating recess, schools have begun to ban certain types of games on the playground. Some elementary schools have banned tag. Others have restricted recess-time soccer and touch football. Educators point to the fear of students hurting themselves or others, or the concern that such activities may escalate into pushing, shoving, or hitting. But just as one of the lessons learned in vigorous play and roughhousing at home with older siblings and parents is when to "cool it" and calm down, and how to control oneself in physical encounters, banning the games in school during recess rather than using them as a learning opportunity could lead to boys having more difficulty knowing how to control themselves, and it may stunt their social development. If a boy doesn't practice learning when to pull back, when to slow down, and when to "cool it," how can he be expected to do it later on when the consequences might be more serious?

In addition to advocating for recess, mothers of boys should actively address the withdrawal of recess as a punishment. If your son's teacher uses denial of recess as a discipline for disruptive behavior, the likely outcome will be an increase in behavior problems. For older students, opting for something physical is often a better punishment than attempting to make them sit still. Rather than having students sitting out a class period in a chair outside the principal's office after a disruptive event in the classroom, my youngest son's school would often have students work in the school office for the period, filing and helping out, which had the added benefit of some one-on-one time with caring adults who were always happy to lend an ear. Since boys communicate well while doing some activity, this helped the boys to open up and talk about what was going on in their lives. It also benefited the school staff, since they became aware of issues in the student's life that might need special attention or intervention.

> "We had an unexpected 90-minute delay for snow. My son spent the extra hour-and-a-half playing outside and shoveling the sidewalk instead of sitting inside watching cartoons, and he was an entirely different child in the classroom that day."
>
> —*Anne, mother of two*

The lack of physical activity caused by the lack of a recess period could also have an impact on your son's classroom behavior and performance.

The Debate over the Single-Sex Classroom

Over the last decade, there's been a growing experiment in single-sex education in our nation. Child psychologists, teachers, and sociologists have posed the question: Is it that our boys are failing at school? Or are our schools failing the boys? Are classrooms led by female teachers, using a teaching style and curriculum that favors the female way of learning and the female style of communication and socialization placing boys at a disadvantage? Is allowing boys a separate learning environment, led by teachers trained in the needs and learning styles of boys, the answer?

An increasing number of states are allowing for at least limited forays into separate classrooms for boys and girls. At the time of this writing, nearly 300 schools across the country were offering at least some single-sex classrooms, and the number is predicted to quickly grow into the thousands. Leonard Sax, the Director of the National Alliance for Single Sex Public Education, highlights the results obtained in one Florida elementary school. At Woodward Elementary School in Deland, Florida, the coeducational classrooms showed boys at a distinct disadvantage, with only 38 percent of boys passing a state writing test as opposed to 57 percent of girls. At the same school, in single-sex classrooms, both the girls and boys showed amazing gains, with 75 percent of girls and 86 percent of boys passing. Other studies corroborate these findings that single-sex education has proven a boon to both boys and girls, with both sexes expressing greater confidence about, interest in, and enjoyment of school.

In an article in the 2002 edition of the *Parents League Review*, Diane J. Hulse examined the advantages of an all-male learning environment and argues that, far from lacking variety and range of expression and opinion from a lack of exposure to females, boys in a boys' school are actually more free to define masculinity. Without girls in the classroom, boys are freer to engage in activities that, in a coeducational classroom, would be defined as "feminine" or "sissy." A boy can freely examine the emotional importance of a poem, join drama class, and enjoy painting or opera without stigma. The all-boy environment is more accepting of a range of masculine behaviors because in that context masculinity is not defined in contrast to the feminine behaviors and interests of girls in the school. "First," she writes, "boys in boys' schools do not get cast as the opposite of girls." Boys are then free of stereotypes, both in terms of their relationships with other boys, as well as with themselves.

An all-boy school or classroom can also teach to the special needs of boys, meeting the boys' higher requirements for physical activity. All-boy schools understand the need for vigorous physical play and often incorporate up to ninety minutes a day for sports and physical activity into every school day. They can also include the more physical, hands-on approach to learning that boys thrive on.

Opponents of single-sex classrooms, such as the American Civil Liberties Union and the American Association of University Women, argue that segregating classrooms by sex will simply be a return to separate but equal education, and that it will open the flood gates to segregation by race or religion, ostensibly in the name of providing education according to the best interests of each group. Beyond that, they also argue that the practice is simply unlawful and discriminatory. Others argue that the all-boy environments are hotbeds of misogyny and intolerance. Some simply feel the research thus far has been inconclusive and more study needs to be done before endorsing single-sex classrooms.

Naturally, every family has to determine for itself whether an all-boy academic environment is right for a specific child, but the opportunities are becoming more and more available, and the research definitely bears some consideration.

Homework Help

Boys have far more problems with homework than do their female classmates. They're less well organized, tend to start the homework later, and once they do start it, they spend less time on the work. They try to do homework in front of the TV, or with a cell phone pressed to their ear talking to a friend, or put off doing the work until the homeroom period the next day and then do a rush job. As discussed earlier in the chapter, boys also tend to have more difficulty putting in a sustained effort. Face it, boys just figure they've got better things to do! But doing homework, and doing a good job of it, is vitally important to academic success. Studies have shown that students who devote more time to homework perform better in school. But homework is often a battle. Few kids come home from a long day of school and dash to the kitchen table, sliding into their chair like a batter taking first base, shouting "Woohoo! Let me at those books!"

In raising my own boys, I faced every sort of homework issue. My kids were the Kings of Procrastination. We did the "Homework? What homework?" routine, the "I did it already" dance, and the "Why should I care about calculus since I'll never use it in real life?" theoretical debate. I saw papers scribbled so quickly it looked like the kid just tied a pen to the dog's tail. I remember squinting at one composition and pointing at a word, asking, "What? What does this say?" and having my son sigh heavily and reply, "Ma, that's my name." Most kids would rather do anything other than sit down and study. So what's a mom to do?

First of all, despite your son's protests that he *needs* to have *Blind Date* blaring on the TV while he's working, the TV needs to go off because it requires too much splitting of attention for the child to concentrate and retain anything he's reading. Music, to a certain degree, doesn't seem to be as much of a distraction, but the volume should be kept reasonable.

You should create a specified study space that's organized and free of clutter. A kitchen table is fine, or a desk in the kid's room or living room. If you can have a space devoted exclusively to homework and projects, it puts your son in the proper frame of mind just sitting down there. Make sure he has a comfortable place to sit (in other words, not the chair everyone hates because it's ugly and uncomfortable). Some studies have shown that kids actually focus and concentrate better reclining slightly, so don't insist he sit up straight if he seems able to focus with his legs up on the table and leaning back in his chair (unless, of course, he's in danger of breaking the chair—I lost four chairs that way). There are a lot of desk chairs that rock and recline slightly avail-able through office supply stores. Especially for a fidgety, high-energy boy, being able to rock may actually help him focus on his work. A few ingenious parents have their active sons sit on the knee-high exercise balls used by gyms. The continual slight movements necessary to keep balanced is enough to allow him to stay seated and working. Be sure to allow your son to take breaks if he's going to be working more than thirty minutes. Homework time should not be turned into a death march, with a "We have to finish this in one seating or die trying" attitude.

Keep whatever supplies he'll need to do homework in the same space. Pens, paper, calculators, a dictionary, a thesaurus, and other necessities should be stored in a drawer or nearby box to avoid wasting time searching for needed items when it's time to work. Make sure the area has sufficient lighting. Ideally, light-ing should come in over the shoulder and not be glaring up or into the child's eyes.

If your son uses a computer to do homework, check regularly to make certain printer paper and ink cartridges are available, and keep spares on hand to prevent the late night "My project is due in the morning and our ink ran out!" calamity.

Try to establish a set time to start homework. Work with your son's particular schedule and rhythms to figure out what time of day during which he works best. For some kids, it's late afternoon after having a chance to play and have a snack after school, and for others, it's right after dinner. If your son is frequently restless at a certain time, don't try doing homework then, and if he often tires early in the evening, or he's unpredictable about when he'll fall asleep, get homework out of the way early on. If someone else is responsible for him during his homework time, go over your expectations with that person.

Keep study time exclusively for studying, no phone calls (other than about homework), and no text-messaging! You may need to ask your son to leave his cell phone in another room during homework if you have a chronic text-messager. If your son has no homework one night, or finishes early, ask him to continue to study quietly, review his work, or do a few extra practice questions. If you have a set period for homework, and your child knows he won't be able to cut it short and go do something else, he'll be less likely to try to rush and do a sloppy or incomplete job.

Be available to help with homework questions, and check your son's homework, not only to be sure it was completed, but also to see that the answers are complete and correct. If you're unavailable during your son's homework time due to work or other obligations, try taking advantage of some of the "homework helpers" listed later in this chapter. While you should help to make certain your son understands how to do the work, *don't do it for him!* Help with a few sample questions, and then back off and let your son try the rest on his own. Don't allow him to whine or cajole you into doing every single problem with him or you'll be hearing "But I don't know how!" every evening for the rest of you son's school career.

If your son has scheduling conflicts, like sports and extracurricular activities, you may need to vary the schedule, but if you find your son unable to keep up with his schoolwork because he doesn't have enough time in his evening, it may be time to cut down on the activities. He may love karate class, but if it's cutting into his ability to do homework, something's got to give, and schoolwork has to have priority. Some parents find their children are able to do their homework in the car on the way to and from activities, but personally, I'm not ready to see children scheduled that tightly, and I prefer to use car time for chatting and finding out what's going on in life. They'll have enough time as grown adults to rush around with every moment scheduled; childhood should have plenty of unscheduled moments and R&R. My best memories of my kids weren't the awards ceremonies or the Tae Kwon Do belt tests (and definitely not the visits to the vice principal's office!), but the moments sitting on the front deck, or out in the backyard, when the impromptu barbecue became an even more impromptu water gun fight, or when we suddenly decide to spend a long, lazy afternoon tubing down the river. Don't let your child be scheduled out of unexpected moments.

■ For more tips on getting your child through his assignments with ease, check out *Home Sweet Homework: A Parent's Guide to Stress-Free Homework & Studying Strategies That Work,* by Sharon Marshall Lockett.

Quite a few parents complain that schools have simply been assigning too much homework in recent years, and I've seen it myself. A rule of thumb many expert educators strive for is ten minutes of homework per grade level as an optimum. So first graders would do ten minutes of homework a day, a sixth grader might do an hour, and a high-school senior may have two hours of studies a night. If your son is getting more than this amount of homework regularly (and it's not excessive delays in completing the assignments that are stretching out the time spent on doing the homework), or if the homework is very irregularly spaced so there are three hours one night of the week and none two others, speak to your son's teacher, and if necessary, rally together with other parents from class to speak as a group. If that doesn't get action, take your concerns to the school board. As discussed earlier, schools and teachers are under pressure from the No Child Left Behind Act to bring up classes' performances on standardized tests, but that doesn't mean parents are powerless to act in their child's best interests. Voice your opposition to any policy or procedure that isn't beneficial to your son, and don't stop rattling cages until you get action!

How can you be sure what your son's homework assignments are? Many schools now post assignments on a class or school Web page, and some teachers have taken the initiative to do so even if it's not regular school policy. If not, try using an assignment notebook (a small spiral pad or bound composition book works best). Have your child write down the assignments in the book and bring the book home daily. If you find your child neglecting to write down the assignments, or writing them down incorrectly, ask the teacher to check your son's notebook daily and initial it. You can then check it daily and initial it as well. The notebook can also be used to jot quick messages to the teacher.

Your child will get his homework done more quickly and efficiently if he's well organized, but he may need some help getting his act together. If he's losing worksheets or not turning in homework the next day because he couldn't find it in his backpack, he definitely needs an organizational system and some coaching in implementing it. A waterproof backpack or messenger bag to keep everything in one place helps. One with separate pockets for pens helps keep books and notebooks from being ruined by the exploding pen or uncapped marker. Use inexpensive pocket folders for completed homework (you can color-coordinate these to match the subject's notebook) and one for signed permission slips or other correspondence so they travel safely back to school and are easy to find and pull out and turn in. New worksheets can be tucked into the same folders for the trip home. Use different colored notebooks for each subject so that your son is less likely to pack the wrong ones to bring home.

Outside Help

School is changing, and moms are confronted with subjects that they never took in school or never did well in themselves. How can you help your son in Spanish when you took French in school? Most of the moms I spoke with in researching this book expressed concern about how to help their son with subjects they lack confidence in themselves, especially math and sciences. Many were looking for relatives and friends with more skills in those subjects willing to pitch in during those times. And, frankly, sometimes it helps to just have a second person assisting with homework since there are times when there's extra stress in the parent-child relationship that seems to rear its head when the parent is called upon to act in the capacity of learning coach. Mom's fatigue, a recent disagreement, or emotional frustrations (particularly during those puzzling periods in early adolescence when kids misread emotional cues or react more emotionally and irrationally) can all add up to moments when it would be better to hand off the homework issue to someone else who isn't so involved with the child on so many levels. Thankfully, there's an ever-increasing number of ways to get free extra help for your son. More and more libraries and school districts are offering free online homework assistance. The King County Library System in King County, Washington, offers assistance to students in grades four through twelve, even those who are home-schooled or in private school, and there's a link for Live Homework Help. The Multnomah County Library in Oregon offers one-on-one tutoring for such diverse subjects as Mythology, Social Issues, and the Mysterious & Unexplained, in addition to the regular Math, History, and Language Arts. The State of Alabama offers "homeworkalabama," a free tutoring service for students in grades four through twelve, and even for introductory college courses. Major Web sites like *www.Jiskha.com* work on a message-board system and allow students to post homework questions and have a team of experts available to post responses. The *www.family*

education.com site offers downloadable Homework Relief Packs that give step-by-step instructions on how to do math lessons, practice sheets, and tip and shortcuts. It also has articles on how to make learning fun, studying tips, and helpful hints on getting your child organized. The Web site *www.Math.com* will help you to relearn the math you took in high school so you can help your child with algebra and geometry, and you can purchase answer guides for most major school math texts with step-by-step explanations on problem solving that will allow you to make certain your child's answers are correct and that he solved the problem using the correct procedure.

Many schools have programs where older students assist and tutor younger students having problems. Most require that your child be falling behind in the subject to qualify, but if that's the case, inquire with your son's teacher or the school's guidance office to see what help is available. There are amazing opportunities to help moms help their sons succeed in school (where were these where we were growing up?). Just choose the options that work best for your family.

Finally, be a role model of learning to your son. When it's time for him to do his homework, engage in quiet activities yourself such as reading, letter writing, or balancing your checkbook. Actively seek to learn new things constantly. Take an online college course, even a non-credit one. Choose educational or enlightening TV show that supports your son's education and ignites his interest in new subjects. The Discovery Channel, the History Channel, the Learning Channel, and even the nightly news can all supplement school learning and make for wonderful opportunities to engage your son in meaningful discussions. Many boys learn extremely well through video and retain a good deal of the information they receive that way.

As a Mom of a Remarkable Boy, you

- Make certain your son gets enough exercise and vigorous physical play so he can focus in class when he needs to;
- Advocate for recess and free play, and discuss with the teacher alternatives to taking away recess when the child has to be disciplined;
- Seek out male teachers, even if your son has to switch classes;
- Ask that your son be seated at the front of the classroom;
- Suggest books, stories, and activities that will be most interesting to your son;
- Encourage the school to bring in male mentors and speakers;
- Fight stereotyping and negative labeling;
- Make certain your son's classroom is boy-friendly, and consider boys-only classrooms or schools if you feel it will benefit your son;
- Provide a quiet, organized place for homework and study, and teach proper study skills and organization skills to your son;
- Stay involved in your son's school throughout his academic career by volunteering, communicating with teacher and staff, and attending meetings and conferences;
- Seek out learning opportunities in everyday life;
- Encourage your son to use the kitchen as a learning laboratory;
- Assist with homework and explain concepts, rather than just checking in to be sure homework is completed;
- Brush up on your own academic and study skills so you can lead by the best example; and
- Take advantage of tutors and school-provided homework help.

CHAPTER 12

Sports

Boys need sports. They require the exertion, the structure, and the challenge that sports offer. Whether it's playing soccer in an organized league, taking martial arts lessons, or participating in a pickup game of basketball on the playground, boys thrive on athletic endeavors. Many child psychologists feel boys simply naturally require the aggressive physical outlet provided by sports.

Boys and Natural Aggression

It's important to recognize that aggression and violence are two different things. The testosterone that makes a boy a boy has a profound influence on his personality, and on how he interacts with others and what he likes to do. Testosterone makes males naturally aggressive, but not naturally violent.

Twenty years ago, psychologists were arguing that boys and girls were basically the same, and the differences we saw were socialized into them. And thus, they argued, those differences could be socialized out of them. Boys' natural aggression was treated as a defect, a product of a violent culture and stereotype that was forced upon them from birth. Boys liked guns, they argued, because they were given guns to play with and were shown war movies and told "this is how boys and men behave." They hit and wrestled, it was believed, because they saw media images of violence, or observed their violent fathers. Parents were instructed to give gender-neutral toys, avoid violent images, and to give boys dolls to encourage their nurturing side.

And this is all well and good, except moms continued to report that their sons still hit and pummeled each other, still leapt off the tallest step they dared, and given a doll, might kiss it and put it to bed one minute and pretend it's a gun and blast at each other the next! Now, naturally, there's a range of behaviors natural to boys. Some are naturally more aggressive than others. I had two boys who were very different from each other. Aaron, the firstborn son, was more daring as a small child. In fact, girlfriends of mine had difficulty babysitting him because, they said, he was like "wrestling an alligator"! He pretended from the age of two to hunt bears in the woods in our yard. My second son, Aric, was much quieter as an infant and toddler, preferring to observe other children playing from a distance, and spending more time playing with the gentler girls. By high school, the two boys' temperaments had reversed. Aaron became much less likely to participate in aggressive play (though he loved aggressive video games), and Aric had been on the wrestling team and found a love for a sport called mud ball, where the boys flooded a field until it was a muddy bog and then played football until everyone was covered in muck. There's no one standard level of aggression, but typically, you'll find males to enjoy and engage in aggressive activities far more often, and with a special enjoyment.

Boys love to challenge each other physically, even to the point of fighting. Moms are often amazed at how, after having a physical altercation, boys can often immediately resume being the best of friends, and often be even closer than they were before the fight! I'm not talking about a bully intimidating your son at school, but two boys who get into a tussle over some perceived slight or insult. They take a few whacks at each other, gain a new respect for each other's bravery and physical ability, and then just start playing again. Watch two professional boxers who stand toe to toe for twelve rounds until they're both bloody and staggering, and then once the final bell rings, throw their arms around each other and hug. Two minutes earlier, they looked to be trying to kill each other, but once the contest was over, they'd gained a new respect for each other.

Sociologist Janet Lever, in her studies on how boys and girls play, found that boys' disputes that arose out of play were very effectively dealt with, and not allowed to interrupt the game. In fact, she found, boys actually appeared to enjoy arguing about the rules as much as they enjoyed playing the game! The rules, the structure and the ritual of play, are very important elements to boys, and something sports provide in abundance. It teaches self-control, teamwork, and how to handle and moderate aggression. It's helpful for socialization, and is also the backdrop of a good deal of adult mentoring. Nothing can quite replace it. In many ways, sports can be a single mom's best ally.

But Why Do Boys Love Sports So Much?

Boys are exhilarated by physical challenges and thrilled by risks. They feel a need to test themselves against each other physically, to prove themselves, to compete, and to win. They love to feel their bodies moving through space, and they particularly relish moving a ball through space. Studies of differing male and female physiology have shown that boys are wired from birth to respond to moving objects, and their eyes are specialized more than girls' to track moving objects. Their brains light up when they're given the chance to test spatial relations to figure out how objects move through space, and sports key into those talents. From as early as just a few months of age, boys are fascinated by moving objects. Balls, trucks, anything they can make move will be particularly interesting to boys.

Games also present the best structure for boy relationships. The side-by-side, shoulder-to-shoulder play, requiring little other interaction, provides an easy comradeship for males. While girls prefer to get together in small groups, interacting intimately and emotionally through talk and confiding in each other, boys prefer large groups that meet for a shared activity. For girls, if there's an activity for them to do together, such as going swimming or taking a bike ride, it's an excuse to get together. For boys, the activity is the whole purpose!

Satisfying Your Son's Need for Physicality

From a very early age, your son is going to need exuberant physical play. Many moms report their male children were much more active than their girls, even from infancy. Later on, in their toddler years, boys are more likely to break things and knock or push things over. In a study of baby boys and baby girls, a baby girl separated from a desired toy by a lightweight barrier of foam blocks tended to give up and cry for help, while a same age baby boy would most often just push the barrier over to get at what he wanted. Young boys love to jump off things, too, using beds, coffee tables, stairs, and the family couch as springboards. As the mother of a boy, you need to be able to keep up, and yet keep things under control!

The mistake many moms make, according to psychologists, is in assuming that normal young boy activity is hyperactivity. It's especially hard for a parent who had a very laid-back first child, especially a female child, and now is coping with a high-energy toddler or young school-age boy. "He's impossible!" a lot of moms will say. "He's into everything, bouncing around, knocking things over! I never had this trouble with my girls!"

Of course, at some point, there is such a thing as too active. A boy who simply cannot sit still, who thrashes wildly, or whose movements seem compulsive, may require the attention of a doctor. But the vast majority of boys are just normally active. It's just, they're not like females! They need you to engage them in rough-housing, wrestling, running, jumping, chasing, and myriad other activities. You need to wear them out and let them exercise both their bodies and their natural aggressive instincts, and on a daily basis. If you can't, for various reasons, you need to find someone else who can help you out in this department. Getting your son together with other boys to play, enrolling him in a play gym or toddler tumbling class, or just getting him outside to climb on monkey bars and roll down a hill or sand dune will help. Winter-time activities like building snow forts, snowball fights, and sled-ding will also provide a terrific physical outlet. But don't expect a boy to play quietly indoors or play comfortably in a small space all the time. Boys need to have access regularly to a large, open space where they can kick balls, throw things, and just generally be "masters of the universe."

But boys do need an outlet for all that energy, and it can either be constructive or destructive. Sports, free play, and fitness classes allow a constructive discharge of pent-up boy energy.

Organized Sports Versus Free Play

Free play has tremendous values for boys. It allows them to exer-cise their imaginations, and be free from restrictions without set goals or scores to keep. According to the "Importance of Play in Promotion Healthy Child Development and Maintaining Strong Parent-Child Bonds," a clinical report released by the American Academy of Pediatrics, play allows children to conquer fears, build confidence, practice decision-making skills, develop their dexterity, just plain have fun. It provides downtime for your son, a break from the schedule of school, homework, and structured activities.

Free play doesn't mean unsupervised play. It's simply less structured. A child can still be playing ball with friends as free play if it's in a backyard or playground away from the more rigid structure of scheduled games, coaches, and referees. Free play can also encompass solo play as long as it's active play rather than a passive pastime like watching TV. There should be some time for free play incorporated into your son's day, every day.

On the other side, organized sports have values all of their own. Boys benefit tremendously from learning a set of rules and sticking to them, and from the discipline required by practices, drills, and structured games. They also encounter new male mentors and role models in the coaches and volunteers who help out. They learn to take constructive criticism and forge a comradeship with the other boys on the team. Organized sports, under the tutelage and guidance of adult males, can provide some of the rites of passage that older boys need in their transition to manhood and can call on a boy to sacrifice himself for the good of the team, providing elements of the mission for the common good that males also thrive on and grow from.

Martial Arts

Marital arts classes can be wonderful for boys, even for those who aren't interested in traditional, organized team sports. They stress discipline, respect, and fitness. They also allow for a safe, structured environment for controlled aggressive play, and the emphasis is on learning self-control. Children can advance at their own pace and can participate either competitively or simply for the sheer fun of it. Some parents fear the classes encourage violence, or may result in their child taking unnecessary risks, like challenging strangers who seem aggressive, but the opposite is true. The teachers emphasize that avoidance of violence is their goal, and that a child who doesn't present himself like a victim, but instead holds himself with confidence and self-mastery, will discourage others from trying to make him a victim. They also teach that a child should never use his training in order to bully another child or instigate a fight.

> "I will try my best as my son gets older to get him involved in sports, although I'm sure my dad will make sure that happens anyway! I'll also make sure my son has men in his life to help him with sports."
>
> —*Eileen, single mother of one toddler-age son*

Naturally, schools and teaching styles vary, so you should visit a school and watch classes in action to be sure you're comfortable with the school's technique. You should also investigate the many varieties of martial arts to find the one you think would be best suited to your child's abilities. Many schools offer family classes so that you can fitness train right along with your son!

Stepping Outside Your Comfort Zone

A lot of the moms I interviewed expressed a certain discomfort with sports. They were never involved with them themselves, and honestly had little interest in them now. They just didn't understand why their sons found sports so fascinating. If they had ever been married, they probably don't understand how their husbands could be so glued to a TV during March Madness (the college basketball championships) or during the World Series. Frankly, many of them expressed, sports are just stupid! I mean, who cares about a bunch of men moving a ball around a field and knocking each other down or throwing a ball through a hoop?

It's okay to feel that way, as long as you keep it to yourself! Just as moms need to understand their son's special masculine traits and interests, moms are allowed to have their own and have those respected. No one's going to expect you to suddenly become a jockette if it's not natural for you, or suddenly find yourself racing home from a social gathering so you don't miss the tip-off in the Bulls game. But as a mom, you need to make an effort to show interest in what your son is interested in, especially if he's actively playing a sport. MomsTeam provides parenting information for mothers of kids involved in sports, and can offer a helpful perspective on how you can be more supportive and a positive influence on your child's sports involvement. Check them out at *www.momsteam.com.*

Learning about the Sports Your Son Plays or Watches

Nothing can be more frustrating to a boy than trying to explain an exciting play he made and then to realize his mother has no clue. Even if she expresses her pride in him, she can't really understand what it means to him or share his excitement. Take the time to learn about the sports your son is playing or watching. A great place to start with the basics is the Web site *www.moms guide.com.* This site provides simple information on the set-up, positions, and rules of the game for most major sports.

> "I do my best to play rough with (my son) whenever I feel strong enough, and he loves it more than anything. I encourage all sports, though he doesn't need much encouragement. I've taken him to watch football games and now support him in following his team. I've supported him in playing for a Sunday league that would be grossly impractical for me, but a friend of his dad has provided the transport."
>
> —*Emily, single mother of one son*

You can also enroll your son to help teach you. Boys adore being asked to talk about something they know about and are good at. Start early on, as your son is beginning in a sport, and learn along with him. You can also ask for help from other parents attending the games. You'll quickly discern the "old hands" on the sidelines.

Making a Point of Attending Sporting Events

If it's at all possible, you should make a point of going to your son's games. I don't think it's a simple coincidence that a great many leading college players have mothers in the stands who may have traveled hundreds of miles to attend an important game. Your support and encouragement mean a great deal to your son. Research has shown that positive parental involvement increases boys' enjoyment of their sports, causes the boys to view their sports performance more positively, and increases the boys' feelings of self-worth. In a nutshell, boys do better, and feel better, when mom shows she cares about their sports.

Groups

If you're looking for more help getting your son involved in sports, or need to find out where to look for safe, structured sports activities, the following groups cover the nation and have a program to suit every need:

The YMCA (Young Men's Christian Association) is no longer strictly based on faith. The Y and its more than 2,600 facilities and diverse activities are open to men, women, and families of all faiths. Some famous Y programs, like midnight basketball, allow for pickup games outside of structured leagues, while their formal sports programs offer training in basketball, volleyball, baseball, softball, T-ball, soccer, and gymnastics. The Y focuses on positive interaction with adult mentors, strong personal values, and character development. Their motto, "We build strong kids, strong families, strong communities," gives you an idea of the Y's commitment to having a positive impact on the whole of the child's life. The Y also has financial assistance policies to ensure that no one is turned away because of an inability to pay. Start your search at *www.ymca.net.*

PAL (the Police Athletic League) has been in existence for more than sixty years and now has more than 400 chapters and more than 1,700 facilities, serving more than two million young people. The group brings together police officers and young people in such activities as boxing, basketball, and baseball leagues. The focus of the PAL is to build respect for the law, law enforcement, and authority. Again, the emphasis is on strong adult male mentorship. Look for a PAL chapter near you by going to *www .nationalpal.org.*

Little League Baseball is a respected national tradition and is now open to both boys and girls between the ages of five and eighteen, and it also has a division for disabled children to participate in. Little League has taken the initiative of initiating the Child Protection Program, which conducts background checks of their volunteers and paid workers—anyone who would have repetitive contact with your child—and they also have a program available to the local leagues that allows parents of players access to a national criminal background check network so you can be more confident of the people you're allowing to interact with your son. The national organization's Web site, with links for local leagues, is *www.littleleague.org.*

Sports Camps

Every year, millions of boys are going to beg to be allowed to go to sports camps. These allow a child to hone his skills, interact with other boys, and experience new styles of coaching and new sports techniques. Offered for nearly every conceivable sport, these camps run anywhere from several days to several weeks, and can be either a local day program or a residential (sleep-away) camp. Some even offer a family camp option where Mom, Dad, an uncle, or even a grandparent can attend and practice their skills along with the child. While the focus is often on high-school-age students, many camps offer beginner programs for children as young as four. Programs typically run anywhere from $200 for a five-day day program to $600 or more for a five-day residential program. While these programs can represent a significant expense, many offer discounted programs and even financial aid programs to families that qualify, so if your child is really serious about a sport or feels improving his sports performance is important to his self-esteem, investigate these options before deciding you can't afford it.

As a Mom of a Remarkable Boy, you

- Understand your boy's need for exuberant physical activity and provide him with outlets;
- Understand your son's natural aggression and don't view it as a defect or flaw;
- Provide your boy with access to organized sports in a safe, structured environment;
- Know your son wants his mom to be interested and involved with his activities;
- Learn the basics of the sports your son plays, so you can converse with him knowledgeably; and
- Also allow time for free play, to encourage creativity and relaxation.

CHAPTER 13

Encouraging Masculinity

In the 1960s and 1970s, many psychologists feared that boys raised by single mothers would be more effeminate, and unable to define and develop their masculine identities without a constant male figure in the home. Thankfully now, with little evidence to really support that theory, most professionals have discarded this notion. Nonetheless, single moms find themselves faced with the lingering fear that they don't know how to teach their sons to be men. Most learn, however, that their sons are capable of teaching their moms all they need to know. All we have to do is listen. The best way to encourage masculinity is to accept it and embrace it in all its many expressions.

One blessing of single motherhood is the opportunity to raise a son free from some of the restrictions and limitations a father in the home might place on the child. How many moms do you know who gladly indulge their young sons' early play with dolls while fathers cringe and try to surreptitiously replace a baby doll with G.I. Joe (clad with all the latest weapons and perhaps a realistic scar)? And how many dads grow impatient with their male child's tears, no matter how young the boy, believing crying to be unmasculine, and pass along a legacy of what psychologist William Pollack calls "The Mask of Masculinity?"

Other males usually place the strictest limitations on what boys are supposed to be like, act like, think like. And it's only natural for our boys to place great importance on the opinion of other boys and of older men. You can't completely control what the outside world is going to present to your son as a model for masculine life. But you can create an atmosphere at home of unlimited possibilities, warm support, and encouragement that will hopefully encourage your child to question, challenge, and even reject those depictions of masculinity that are destructive, constraining, and emotionally crippling to men.

By having the freedom to allow and encourage your son to express his own interests, in his own way, and to fully experience and accept his own emotions, single moms are giving rise to a new, broader definition of masculinity, without the rigid stereotypes and conformity.

> "I have been very liberal and open with my son—allowing him to play and do what he wants to try. He was not pushed towards masculine things but has gravitated there himself over time. He played dress up and with dolls and stuffed animals as a toddler (my own father was not thrilled about it but did not have a say in it). Both my mother and I have been more open to my son playing with and exploring all things."
>
> —Debbie, single mother of one son,
> now married with a second son

Being masculine today can incorporate both strength and tenderness, both the artist and the architect, both the warrior and the work-from-home dad. By simply acknowledging that all of these traits can be part of being a man, and that they are all good, positive masculine ideals, your son will be a more secure and confident male with a much less narrowly defined notion of what life will hold in store for him.

Encourage your son to see untraditional male characteristics in a positive light. Point out everyday examples from your community, from the news, and even from entertainment media to highlight the widening definition of what manliness is. We had a lively discussion around our dinner table when a famous professional wrestler, someone everyone viewed as very tough and manly, began to decline to do shows that required too much travel so that he could stay home more with his wife and new baby. We had a very serious discussion after watching Court TV and seeing interviews with male sheriffs investigating a murder, and seeing these men cry quite openly for the victims though they'd never known them in life. So often one sees a fictional depiction of the callous law enforcement officer as untouched and unfeeling, the "strong, silent male." Realizing that there's a balance, that real strong men can cry and feel pain and admit to it, was very beneficial to my sons and gave them a new regard for the people involved in this challenging field.

At the same time, combat the negative stereotypes. Question any limitations placed, either explicitly or more implicitly, on what activities, interests, or occupations your son wishes to explore or participate in. Is your son more interested in the flute than the saxophone? Don't let your school's band director discourage him! Instead, find him examples to encourage his interests.

Challenge movie and TV depictions of leading men who are disrespectful of their relationships with women. Rather than accepting that this behavior is "cool" or "macho," begin a discussion of how this attitude and behavior ruins lives and families, and how in the long run it is hurtful even to that "macho" male. At the same time, point out real life role models of caring, involved men who respect and support females.

Accepting and Appreciating Our Sons' Maleness

In so many ways and for so many reasons, boys are simply different from girls. They are different from us, their mothers. Those differences are reflected not only in physiology, but also in temperament, communication style, and relationship dynamics. Those differences can be reflected right down to what colors they prefer, what perspective they use in drawing a picture, or what volume they turn the radio to. It's so tempting at times to suggest a different way of doing things, to allow our own feminine tastes to judge what our sons do, think, and prefer, and to find them foreign and hard to comprehend. But as we learned ourselves in our own lives, when an alternate way of doing something is suggested, it's often interpreted as a criticism, or as a rejection.

Ever have an encounter with a mother or mother-in-law who looked over your shoulder while you were cooking and said, "Gee, dear, you might want to think about adding some rosemary to that chicken" or something similar? How did that feel? Did it feel like you were being told that your way of doing something was wrong? Now consider that in relation to your exchanges with your son. Do you ever find yourself suggesting alternatives that would be most to your taste?

Of course, it's perfectly fine to suggest other ways of doing things when it comes to practical matters, like when to do homework. But when it comes to issues of personal expression, keep an open mind.

Watching Our Words

I recall sitting with a girlfriend and her young son one day and watching my friend losing it with her son's boisterous play. It was a rainy day and the boy had been cooped up and was just bursting with energy, while his older sister was quietly engaged in some art project at another table. Finally, my friend just blew up at her son, asking him "Why can't you just play quietly like your sister!" The boy stopped what he was doing and looked up, stricken. "Do you wish I was a girl, Mommy?" he asked, near to tears. It seemed the Earth stopped spinning for a moment while my friend realized the impact of her words. She pulled him in close to her and hugged him tight, tears running down her own face, telling him over and over again that she was sorry and she was wrong and she was so very glad he was a boy. The moment really opened my friend's eyes to the way her words could be interpreted as a rejection of her son's masculine self. She made more of an effort to realize her son's different needs, and went out of her way to find him ways to burn off his excess energy and engage him on days when he couldn't play outside in the yard.

We must also be aware of any lingering conflicts we ourselves have with men that can color our exchanges with our sons. Is your son overhearing you tell a girlfriend that some guy who is acting like a jerk is "just like a man"? Do you get cut off in traffic and slam your palm on your steering wheel and exclaim "Men!"? Or has your son ever done something annoying and have you tell him "You're just like your father!"? Try to catch yourself before you male bash, not only in front of your child, but any time, since it becomes a habit that's hard to break. You're fighting stereotypes here, so don't reinforce them! Never say anything that will make your son ashamed of his identity as a male. If you slip up, immediately discuss what happened with your son and explain that you were wrong, and why you said what you did. If you're mad, you're mad at one person, not a whole gender!

It Doesn't Have to Be Our Way

As so many moms have discovered, often what emerges as our son's personality is sometimes confusing to us. Mom may be strongly anti-gun and trying hard to develop her son's nurturing side, yet every time she turns around, he's diving over the couch pretending to be in a shootout with bad guys. Mom might buy her son a paint set or markers to encourage him to draw and find he's only used the black, silver, and blue (and maybe a little red to show explosions) and has created scene after scene depicting an intergalactic war with spaceships blasting each other. Does this mean your son has tremendous underlying aggressions, or is actually some sort of violent felon in the making? Should you work to try to stamp out all this "hostility" and make him "play nice"? Certainly not! All of these are simply normal male behavior, and need to be appreciated. Rather than suggest that it would be so much nicer to perhaps draw a house and people or the family pet, engage your son in a discussion of what's going on in the picture he's drawing. Don't react negatively or ask him (with that concerned-mom voice) why he only draws battles. Praise his creativity.

> "They (my sons) naturally do 'boy' things, such as fighting, liking violent games on Playstation and computer games, liking swords and other play weapons, liking sports. This all came naturally."
>
> —*Deborah, single mom of two sons*

Your son will likely be louder, livelier, and more boisterous than a girl the same age. He needs to be allowed and encouraged to run, jump, shout, and just generally "be a boy," though it's perfectly reasonable to limit those expressions to certain times and places, as long as he gets those times and those places.

At the same time, don't push a boy who is naturally just quieter to engage in the same loud, exuberant play you see his classmates engaged in. It's also perfectly acceptable for a boy to prefer books to basketball, or chess to skateboarding. Again, allowing for a wide range of personal expression, finding it all perfectly acceptable, and finding things to praise and extol about your son's choices gives him more confidence and self-esteem.

Point out the things that make him unique, and express your pride in him. He might want to spend hours studying a bug colony moving across the sidewalk (as long as they're not on the march to your house). Rather than shuddering and telling him "I hate bugs," ask him what he learned and tell him you're impressed by his powers of observation and his patience, and then encourage him to look up more information on the Internet or from a book from the library.

Wherever your son is on the spectrum of expression, it's important for him to know that you support him, encourage him, love and accept him, and that you're immensely pleased and proud to be raising a boy.

Letting Masculinity Emerge Naturally

Above all, what I learned from other single moms is that masculinity comes naturally to boys. It's not something that we have to teach, train, or bestow. Behaviors that are taught, such as respect for women and self-respect, are universal, not just masculine traits. Good manners, good citizenship, responsibility, courage, loyalty, hard work, honesty, and compassion define human beings, not just men. By modeling those behaviors ourselves, and by pointing out those attributes in others, both male and female, we communicate to our sons the way we want them to live their lives, our expectations and our dreams for them.

> "I'm not sure a boy needs to be parented by a man to learn about manhood/masculinity. My son's picked up the basics very well without! In fact, he seems to have had them within, and got no explicit help for them to surface."
>
> —*Emily, single mom of one son*

By simply listening to our sons, respecting who they are and the way they are, by encouraging them and praising them, and by loving them fully and without reservation as boys as well as children, our sons will be a new generation of truly masculine men, without borders or boundaries, and capable of doing and being anything they want to be.

> "I don't think that becoming a successful caring man/person is about having one male role model. Rather it is the sum of all the positive and negative experiences with the people you love and love you in your life. When defining positive male role models, we must be careful to say which qualities that they exhibit are unique to men and not exhibited by women. Maleness is genetic. In spite of being surrounded mostly by women, my son is all boy, the way my brothers were, growing up a generation ago in the traditional setting. It does come naturally. He's also learning by watching other boys in school and after school."
>
> —*Angela, single mother of one son*

As a Mom of a Remarkable Boy, you

- Understand that there are many expressions of masculinity, and do not confine your son's maleness to a narrow definition;
- Encourage, rather than force, the development of your son's masculine identity;
- Reject and encourage your son to reject people who ridicule or constrain him from a full range of expression;
- Know that gender identity does not mean gender conformity;
- Accept and appreciate masculinity as something separate and unique, not wrong or something to be controlled or subdued;

- Are careful not to male-bash or cause your son shame over his male identity; and
- Relax, because you know that your son's true self will emerge naturally, and that with love, openness, and understanding, a boy will successfully define himself.

CHAPTER 14

Taking Care of Yourself to Take Care of Your Child

No doubt about it, parenting is demanding. Going it alone isn't just harder; there are times when it seems downright nearly impossible. Nearly every solo mother I've met has confessed to at least one desperate phone call to a girlfriend that went something along the lines of "I just can't take it anymore!"

Caring for Your Mental Health

Single moms more than anyone need to be alert to their emotional health and to seek help when they feel overwhelmed, anxious, or depressed. Negative emotions can impair your ability to parent effectively, and can sap you of the precious energy reserves you need for the demands of your hectic life. Don't think you have to wait until you're in a crisis to seek input from a mental health professional, though. While it's great to know you can always access help in an emergency, developing a relationship with a professional now can help you learn coping strategies, manage your stress, deal with conflicts, and develop a healthy parenting style. And don't feel that a tight family budget means you can't possibly afford counseling. Many communities have a mental health services department that offers counseling on a sliding-scale payment basis depending on income, so check with your local health department to see what's available in your area. Many health insurance policies also cover mental health issues, and quite a few employers offer referrals to counseling for such issues as stress, anxiety, and depression, as well as problems like gambling and drug and alcohol abuse as part of their services. Ask your employer if they have an EAP (Employee Assistance Plan).

A great place to start your search for services for yourself, your child, or your whole family is the U.S. Department of Health and Human Services National Mental Health Information Center at *www.mentalhealth.gov.* This amazing Web site has directories and links to local mental health services providers throughout the country, as well as a wealth of information on mental health programs and downloadable articles and tips on managing anxiety and other problems.

"I hadn't realized what I was experiencing was depression. The stress of the divorce, financial concerns, and troubles my sons were having adjusting all just built up until I was overwhelmed. I could barely drag myself out of bed, and I had no motivation at work. I was getting sick all the time and my joints ached. Luckily, my doctor asked what else was going on in my life other than just the symptoms I came in for, and he suggested a treatment plan for depression and anxiety. Within weeks, I started to feel better. I still had a lot of issues to contend with, but at least now I felt I could handle it rather than feeling ready to give up."

—*Anne, mother of two sons and a daughter*

Counseling can take many forms so you can choose the style that suits your own needs. You may opt for a traditional one-on-one patient and therapist relationship with a counselor specializing in family issues. There are also group sessions available where you can meet with other people in similar circumstances and help each other work through problems, offer support, and find solutions and coping strategies. Don't be afraid or ashamed to access the services you need. It's not weak to admit you need help; instead it's emotionally mature and insightful to seek to take care of yourself as well as you can so that you can do the best possible for your child. It should be something you feel proud of. Being proactive means you're taking better care of yourself and your son.

Don't hesitate to ask to be evaluated for depression. Undiagnosed depression can make it so much harder to move forward effectively with your life, as well as to parent effectively, and that can increase your child's likelihood of suffering from adjustment problems and to act out later on. A study published in *Social Psychiatry and Psychiatric Epidemiology* noted that single moms have a higher incidence of depression and stress, and suffered from isolation, with fewer social contacts. But you can take action to reduce your stress and establish a support system to provide the nurturing, comfort, and mentoring a single mom really needs.

Symptoms of Depression:

- Lack of interest in your normal activities and hobbies
- Inability to concentrate or think clearly
- Weight change, either up or down
- Loss or increase in appetite or change in eating habits
- Difficulty sleeping, or sleeping more
- Unexplained aches or pains, such as joint or muscle pain, headaches, abdominal pain
- Feeling hopeless
- Feeling that life isn't worth living

- Difficulty performing even normal household tasks, work, or personal responsibilities
- Fatigue
- Despair

Women suffer from depression twice as often as men, and separated and divorced people are more likely than married people to experience depression at some time. I experienced a serious depression myself during the highly conflicted period leading up to my divorce, and would occasionally struggle with it afterward, particularly when I was dealing with some contentious issue in family court. I realized early on that I wasn't the only one suffering, it was impacting my kids, too. Getting help and feeling better wasn't a luxury, it was a necessity.

> "I wouldn't accept the fact that I was depressed. Then my mother pointed out to me that I was expressing a great deal of negativity about my life. She asked me to tell her one happy or uplifting story about something that's happened since my divorce, and I couldn't think of anything. I just never wanted to think of myself as a depressed person. Worse, I was worried how the kids' father might use that against me if he ever found out."
>
> —*Anonymous, mother of two boys*

For moms used to doing for everyone else first and never taking care of their own needs, the idea of putting their own need first can take some getting used to. They always want to put off until there's time. But as a single mother with a child, the only time is going to be time you intentionally schedule for that purpose. Make taking care of your emotional health a priority.

Learning to Say "No"

Are you one of the countless women who find themselves being called upon to help with everything? Do you find yourself taking care of everyone, and receiving very little care back in return? Do you feel like you're running on empty?

Most single moms spend their days feeling frazzled and over-taxed by the demands of home, child, and work. It gets even worse if your son's schedule includes a lot of extracurricular activities, or if you're trying to take a class or two yourself to further your career. Add to that the demands of aging parents, volunteering, friends who want your help, and countless other requests for your time, both large and small, and for many moms, sleep becomes but a fond memory, and the stress level skyrockets. So why do you find yourself continuing to say "yes"?

It's essential to prioritize the demands on your time. Which are must-dos and which are not necessarily necessary? A friend of mine always replies to any complaint about too many obligations by asking "What will happen if you don't do it?" Is it necessary for you, personally, to perform the task or meet the obligation, or can someone else do it? Is there perhaps a more comfortable way to meet the obligation? Can you share the obligation with someone?

"I spent ten years taking care of my mother, having her live in with me and my children, and my siblings were all perfectly content to allow me to do everything without any help. Finally, I had to move to a new area where housing was more expensive and getting a place with enough room for another person was going to be a huge financial strain. Rather than straining to juggle my budget to make it work, I called my brother, who had a spare bedroom in his house, and suggested rather strongly that it was his turn to pitch in and help."

—*Anne, mother of two sons and one daughter*

Sometimes it's uncomfortable trusting other people to do what you've always done yourself. What if they forget, or just plain "do it wrong?" If you're always the one your parents call when they need a ride to the doctor because your sister was always "the flighty one," it's time to make someone else live up to an adult's responsibility. It's too easy for others to allow you to be "the dependable one."

Make other people aware of how demanding your schedule is. Too often, other people take for granted that you've got lots of free time or are simply unaware of the number of obligations you're already juggling. Is it absolutely necessary for you to make Thanksgiving dinner for your entire family without any help just because you always have, or is it time for one of your siblings to take over the responsibility?

> "Your primary obligation is your child's welfare and needs. Your child must come first in your life. Once that is established, the rest will come naturally."
>
> —*Deborah, single mom of two boys*

No matter what it is you're asked or expected to do, think first of the impact on you and your son. Reject the notion that as a woman, and a mother, you're supposed to be unquestioningly giving, helpful, and unselfish. Don't allow others to constantly place you in a service role. You have to take care of yourself first before you can possibly take care of your child.

Taking Care of Your Physical Health

It's important to not ignore your own personal fitness while dealing with the issues of single parenting. Emotional health and physical health go hand in hand, and study after study touts the surprising mental benefits of exercise. You'll find it's a great stress-reliever, combats depression, and even fights fatigue. A study published in the April 2001 edition of the *British Journal of Sports Medicine* showed that for some patients, exercise was even more effective than medication in fighting depression! Exercise gives you a break from the day's worries, helps you sleep better at night, and helps keep off extra pounds. Instead of reaching for that box of chocolates the next time your nerves are on edge, reach for your sneakers instead!

Too often, moms in a time crunch let their own fitness slide, even if they're being diligent about making sure their sons get the proper exercise. Sure, you know it's important, and you might even be looking forward to the day when your life becomes less demanding and you can get back into the swings of things, but right now, you can't even imagine it. You may even think you just don't have the energy to exercise! Especially if you're dragging yourself through your day, falling asleep on the couch as soon as the demands of the day are through, how can you possibly think you'll have the energy to do more? The surprising thing is, exercise actually gives you more energy! By making your cardiovascular system more fit, you'll be delivering more of the oxygen your body needs for energy, both during exercise and while resting. And by making your muscles stronger and building endurance, you won't become as exhausted by normal daily activity. You also have too much to risk to not make fitness a part of your daily routine.

Exercising with your son has multiple benefits. Not only are both you and your child keeping healthy, you're building opportunities for communication and interaction, and setting a good example of physical fitness.

Walking, jogging, and running together are extremely easy to do anywhere and don't require expensive equipment or classes. These activities can also be done even with a very young child. Hiking in the woods or parks can allow for a more leisurely pace and can be combined with some educational activities, like identifying trees, birds, and animals. Saturdays and Sundays in our mountain town bring out dozens of canoes and kayaks on the river, and boating is a perfect combination of exercise and relaxation and ideal for pairs or small groups. If you're nervous about a tippy boat like a canoe, try renting a small rowboat or an inflatable raft, but be sure no matter what type of craft you're in, everyone is wearing a proper life vest.

If there's one near you, try a spin at a good, old-fashioned roller skating rink, or strap on ice skates for some winter fun. Doing some of the physical activities you did when you were a kid yourself will keep you young at heart, and heart-strong.

Right now, about 70 percent of American women aren't getting enough exercise, and it's taking a huge toll. Cardiovascular disease is now the number one killer of women age thirty-five and over, and inactivity doubles a person's risk for heart disease. The American Heart Association lists physical activity as just as important for heart health as controlling blood pressure and serum cholesterol and not smoking.

If it's been a while since you exercised, you should first check with your doctor before starting any fitness routine. Then, start slowly. The Women's Heart Foundation recommends starting with a ten-minute workout and then adding two minutes a week until you reach your goal. Trying to ramp up your exercise too quickly may result in any injury or other complication that will only result in discouraging you.

Walking is great exercise that's available anywhere, anytime, and other than getting a good pair of walking shoes, it's free! Dr. Steven Pratt, author of *SuperFoods Healthstyle*, recommends using a simple pedometer, a device that clips onto your waistband and measures how many steps you take, as a way to keep track of how much walking you do. He suggests a daily goal of 10,000 steps, which is actually about twice as many as the average person gets in our sedentary society. It sounds like a huge number, but you'll be surprised how quickly and easily it adds up. And using a pedometer can actually encourage you to walk further, since it gives you an easy measure of your progress, and you'll find yourself looking for little ways to bring that daily number just a little higher. Instead of driving around looking for the nearest parking space, park at the far end and walk. Rather than pushing a button and waiting for the elevator, head for the stairs instead.

One of the single moms I met works at a high school and packs a pair of sneakers in her bag every day and spends half of her lunch hour walking around the quarter-mile track just outside the school gym. She figures she's probably able to log a mile of walking a day that way, and she's working on increasing her pace so she can do even more. Swinging your arms, using light ankle weights, and listening to upbeat, fast-paced music on headphones can make your walking workout more productive and enjoyable. Getting fit can be as simple as just getting out of your own front door!

You can double your motivation to walk by pairing up with another mother for a daily power walk. Even ten minutes a day in the fresh air can elevate your mood, and twenty minutes a day of sustained exercise has significant health benefits, helping with cardiac health, blood pressure, and weight maintenance. With both infant carriers and backpacks available, as well as jogging strollers, even moms with tiny tots can pack up the kids and hit the walking path. Gyms and YMCAs also offer Mommy and Me exercise classes that allow you to interact with your youngster while toning your muscles and meeting other parents. And as I mentioned in Chapter 12 on sports, the Y has a policy that no one is ever turned away for an inability to pay, so family finances are no obstacle to family fitness.

The stress-relieving aspect of exercise is a major boon for single moms. Moderate exercise (enough to cause you to break into a light sweat) causes the body to release endorphins, which in turn cause you to feel calm and relaxed. Stress, by itself, can be exhausting. It clutters our minds and keeps us from thinking clearly, it interferes with sleep, it makes us impatient with the people in our lives, and it damages our health. By increasing the level of the stress hormone, cortisol, which causes belly weight gain, stress can even make us fat! Work in some stress-relieving exercise as part of your daily schedule.

Yoga

Yoga, in its many forms like Hatha yoga and Yinyasa, uses a series of postures that stretch and tone your muscles and increase your strength and stamina. Yoga has been shown to be very effective at combating stress and has been linked to being beneficial in the management of other problems like back pain, depression, and chronic headaches. Some people think that in order to benefit from yoga you have to hold certain spiritual beliefs, or live a very New Age lifestyle, but that simply isn't true. While some people choose to practice yoga as part of a deeper spiritual quest, many participate simply for the physical and health benefits. Yoga has been shown to be great for kids, helping them to relax and teaching them good responses to feelings of stress and anxiety. It's even been shown to help with children who suffer from hyperactivity or ADD (attention deficit disorder).

Yoga forces you out of your head, so you lose (for at least a little while) your preoccupation with your problems and your worries. It's excellent for unwinding and gives you a greater sense of self-control and control over your body.

If you're a beginner to yoga, you'll probably want to start with Hatha yoga, which is slow paced and gentle, and teaches the basic yoga poses. Some gyms also now teach a style called "power yoga," which is very demanding physically, for those with some yoga background who are looking for a more strenuous workout. For a nice overview of yoga and information on how to begin practicing yoga, visit *www.yoga.about.com*.

Making Time for Yourself

It's important to make some time just for yourself. You shouldn't use every spare moment that the children are out of the house on visitation or with friends and relatives just to try to complete all the chores you have difficulty getting done while the kids are home. It's so very tempting to run around like a wild woman the second the house is empty, running errands, doing housework, and getting caught up on your paperwork. But it's also soul-draining to not spend at least a portion of that time doing things that are simply and exclusively for your pleasure. With effective time management, you can still get the house in order and still make time to indulge yourself in some refreshing activities.

If you love reading, reward yourself for completing a particularly difficult task with a half-hour soak in the tub with a good book. If you have to drive all over town to do groceries, pick up the cleaning and go to the bank, stop for fifteen minutes at a pretty local café or coffee shop that offers a pleasant view or sidewalk tables, and enjoy a bottle of spring water or cup of herbal tea. If you're scheduled to drive to pick up the children from their grandparents' house, leave a little early and stop at a park or nature preserve along the way and take a leisurely walk to observe the changing seasons. A few brief moments engaged in doing things that refresh your soul and reward your senses will allow you to come back to your parenting and household duties with renewed vigor and energy.

Reward Yourself Moments. Schedule to include one of these ten- to fifteen-minute escapes into your day:

- Put on some of your favorite music and dance, dance, dance. You'll improve your mood and boost your metabolism at the same time. It's a great release!
- Listen to a comedy routine on CD, tape, or online. A ten-minute belly laugh is great for your heart, lowers your

blood pressure and stress hormones, and actually aids your immune system!

- Log onto one of the online moms' message boards or chat rooms listed in the appendix of this book, and make a new friend.
- Take a brisk walk around the block. Walking helps to clear your mind and relax you while helping with weight maintenance and cardio health. You'll gain the added benefit of meeting your neighbors and gaining more sense of community. Having a dog gives you an extra excuse to fit in a walk, and is a great ice-breaker with new people. My pet Bassett Hound is the hit of the neighborhood and is always ready to make the rounds and get her daily dose of belly rubs and ear scratches.
- Catch up on your favorite hobby. While you might think that knitting, sewing, or scrapbooking take too much time for you, even if you can only devote fifteen minutes to it twice a week, that's twenty-six hours a year!
- Call an old friend or a relative whom you haven't spoken to in a while. It's so easy to lose track of the people in our lives when we're really busy, so work to reverse your narrowing circle of contacts. Especially for a single mom, it's vital to keep in touch and keep your social and support network strong
- Practice a series of yoga stretches. Don't think you have to be a hard body in spandex to perform a basic yoga routine. If it's been a while since you've exercised, check with your doctor first and start slowly to avoid injury. The idea is to aid your relaxation and flexibility, so if something hurts, stop.
- Spend a few minutes in reflection of everything you have to be grateful and happy about.

Calming Exercises for Moms

Being able to control your stress is important for many reasons. Both your mental and physical health are impacted by your stress level, and stress directly impairs your ability to parent effectively. The next time you feel stressed, try one of these calming routines. Better yet, work them into your regular routine to help avoid stress and its negative effects.

Deep Breathing

If it feels like you're absolutely ready to melt down, try stepping away (physically if you can, in your mind if you can't!), close your eyes, clear your mind, and take a deep breath. Unless whatever mayhem is happening involves fire or blood, it can wait a moment. Fill your lungs fully, and feel your muscles begin to relax. Hold the breath for three seconds and then slowly release the breath through your mouth to a count of ten. Push the air from your lungs fully. Repeat.

The mere act of suspending your thoughts, words, and actions for a half minute will help put things in perspective.

Relaxing the Mind

Close your eyes and clear your mind. Breathe normally and repeat to yourself silently a calming word or reaffirming word or phrase with each exhalation. You might use "calm," "peace," or "loved." I also use the word "found," which resonates with me. Over time, you'll find the words which work best for you. Continue to focus on your breathing and on repeating your word, slowly, calmly, keeping your mind free of distractions and worries.

Progressive Muscle Relaxation

An extremely common and popular technique for inducing relaxation developed by Edmund Jacobson in the 1930s, Progressive

Muscle Relaxation (PMR) involves deliberately and consciously tensing and then relaxing specific muscle groups in sequence. This can be done either sitting in a chair, or lying on a bed or mat, and can even be done in bed as you settle in to sleep. Focus on one muscle group at a time, intentionally tensing the muscles in that area, hold the tension for five to ten seconds, and then completely release the tension, feeling the muscles relax and go limp. Start working with one foot, then your lower leg and foot, then your entire leg, before shifting to the other side. Afterwards, progress to your hand, then forearm and hand, and then your entire arm, and again, switch to the other side. Finally, you should work your way up your trunk, tensing and relaxing first your abdomen, then your chest, and lastly, your neck and shoulders and then your face. There's an excellent explanation of the full process at the Web site *www.guidetopsychology.com*.

Moving on with a New Love Interest

An important aspect of taking care of yourself is allowing yourself the full range of human relationships. You need love, warmth, and companionship. But as a single mom, you have special concerns. How do I know when to introduce a new man to my son? What effect will my dating have on my relationship with my child? Is this new man trustworthy around children?

The first hard and fast rule is to go slow in introducing new men. Wait until you feel certain the relationship will be a long-term one. Don't introduce someone you're just testing the waters with, or are just going out with for a bit of fun and socialization. Your son needs a sense of security and stability. He could become attached to what turns out to be a temporary love interest. It's also best to introduce the new person as your friend, though older children and teens are usually pretty astute as to what the real story is. But it's a good time to teach them that the best relationships grow out of friendships.

The first three people I encountered when I began dating again after my separation are perfect examples of why you don't want to introduce your child too quickly. The first one intentionally took me to a club he knew his ex would be at, hoping for a confrontation. The second had nearly his entire extended family surreptitiously stashed at tables throughout the restaurant we went to so they could "check out" the new woman and give him their verdicts (I didn't wait around to see if I was "voted off the island"!). And the third, whom I met only for a brief preliminary coffee date, ran the date like a job interview and declared that the space between my front teeth "just *has* to be fixed!" That one's probably still waiting at the Starbucks for me to come back from the ladies' room. And these were all well-educated, professional men, with sons of their own, and they seemed, at least on the surface, to be reasonably normal adults.

Obviously, be cautious about excessive displays of affection in front of your child, and be wary of a man who won't respect that boundary! Some men try to test moms by pushing them a bit in front of their children, in a way of demanding "well, who are you going to consider? Me or your kid?" Any man who tries to make you put him first in front of your child, especially a man you've only recently gotten serious with, is bad news!

That's not to say you shouldn't be considerate of everyone's feelings, both adult and child. If your son is overtly rude to your new guy, he definitely needs to be called on it. And chances are likely this could occur. Boys sometimes become quite nasty to their moms, as well, when the mother begins dating again. Especially if your son harbors a fantasy of getting you and his dad back together again (which is extremely common, even years after a divorce), he's going to want this new man out of the picture! Be understanding of where your son is coming from. As far as your son is concerned, your already limited time and availability is being further reduced by this new person's appearance. Be reassuring, and continue to stress the reality that you and your ex are not going to get back together no matter what. Spend some special time alone with your son, and don't forego cherished family traditions. If you've always had Friday night as family movie night, don't change that. Your new guy has got to understand that your son has priority in your life, and anyone who can't accept your obligations as a mom isn't a fit partner for you.

Don't use your son as a confidant. Especially as kids move into their teens and can begin relating in a more adult fashion, it's tempting to tell him things best left unsaid, or to involve him in your personal affairs. Don't. That's thrusting the child into the role of an adult, and beyond that, into a role of caregiver for you. Be especially careful to leave him out of disagreements with your new love interest. While you might be airing a temporary grievance with your new guy that will resolve itself, you could be building a long-term resentment against him if your son know of hurts (whether real or perceived) that will kick his protectiveness into high gear. While you realize disagreements and misunderstandings are part of dating, your son only knows mom's hurting, and that man caused it.

There are some rules the new man has to live by, too, experts suggest. He shouldn't try to take dad's place, though he should definitely model respect for you and insist on it in your son. It's perfectly acceptable for him to tell your son that your son needs to speak to you politely if your child's acting rudely (in fact, all adult males in your son's life should reinforce this constantly), but your new guy can't tell your son to go to his room. That's your place. He cannot walk in and attempt to be an authority figure. While your son should respect all adults, a new adult male still has to earn his trust, and boys won't accept rules or discipline from someone they don't trust and believe in. It's tempting, especially if a mom's going through a difficult time with her son, to try to turn over the discipline angle to another adult, but in those cases, it should be a close male family member he knows well and trusts, like a favorite uncle or grandparent, not a new man who is still forming a relationship with you and your child.

He also shouldn't try to force a close relationship with your son too quickly. Let your son set the pace. He'll let you know when he's ready for more interaction. And let your new man and your son have a relationship of their own and find their own level. I was absolutely delighted when I came home one day to find my significant other had arrived early and took the opportunity to start dinner on the grill. My sons, drawn by the "man activity" of mixing fire and meat, came out to help, and by the time I arrived, the three of them were eating right off the grill using two-foot long barbecue forks. My sons grinned wildly as my boyfriend beat his chest like Tarzan and playfully declared, "We're eating like *real* men, blood dripping from our clenched teeth!" The shared activity and inclusion of my sons in the category of men was something very meaningful to the boys, and it helped take their relationship with my boyfriend to a much deeper level. And yes, they did think to save me a piece!

As a Mom of a Remarkable Boy, you

- Understand that in order to take care of your son, you must first take care of yourself;
- Are proactive about your emotional health, and seek the help you need;
- Work fitness into your own daily routines in ways both big and small;
- Take time for yourself, knowing that way you'll have more to give to others;
- Use calming exercises to reduce stress and combat anxiety; and
- Understand the special needs of your child when you begin dating again.

The Most Important Role Model: You

I n the writing of this book, I was at first excited because of my passion for the subject. My experiences with my own two sons, and my grandsons, and the many boys who'd come to share our home and be part of our family, gave me tremendous hope. Not only could moms raise boys alone, I knew, but it could be hugely rewarding, emotionally gratifying, and yes, even fun.

Then, as I began to do my more formal research in preparation, I was struck with awe, and then humbled. There was so very much new I had to learn, and the field of gender studies was exploding. No sooner had I devoured one study when a new one came along that took the subject even further that challenged preconceptions even more deeply. Information is flooding in, from medical journals and psychology conferences, from educational studies, and even census and population statistics.

This is truly a wonderful time to be a single mom of a boy. Myths and fallacies that had held mothers back, that made moms insecure and unsure, that unfairly placed blame on single mothers and negative stereotypes on fatherless boys, these are, one by one, being examined and discarded. The emerging field of brain science is finally granting acceptability and credibility to what mothers have known all along: Boys are different. Rather than being looked upon as defective girls, where boys' behavior, learning style, manner of communicating, and emotional expression were all considered "wrong," boys are now regaining the understanding and support they had lost in recent years. I'm excited for the future of boys, and for their moms.

And I met some amazing moms in creating this project. They were funny, brave, creative, inventive, tireless, and utterly devoted to their families. They were also challenged by finances, child-care issues, uncooperative schools, immense demands on their time and emotional resources, and worries for their sons. But they persevered and created success out of chaos. Often, these women had to create lives for themselves and their sons out of the ashes of divorce. They had to overcome emotional scars of abuse while healing their sons at the same time. No job could ever have been so important or meaningful. I'm awestruck.

Creating a New World

The most encouraging part is that single moms are no longer viewing their futures as limited, or their prospects as being defined by their status. While single moms still struggle economically more than other families, they are making tremendous strides in creating financial security for themselves and their children. More and more, they're opting to return to school, or to stay in school. They're taking jobs once considered the domain of men, earning for themselves the higher wages and generous benefits once thought necessary only for the family man. You'll find single moms sweating on road crews with the Department of Transportation, enlisted in the National Guard, and occupying the front offices of giant national corporations. And in expanding their own horizons, these women are creating new possibilities for their sons, and instilling a new mindset in America.

"I can certainly provide a wide variety of modes/models for my son, as caregiver, worker, homemaker, gardener, driver, organizer, fixer, swimmer, cook, cyclist, skier—not all on the feminine spectrum."

—Emily, single mother of one son

Women have always been creative in finding ways to provide for their families and make a home, no matter where they are. That creativity and drive to provide has been the driving force behind single moms starting small businesses that are designed around their lifestyle, and making them successful. Single mothers are applying for patents, copyrights, and trademarks in record numbers. They're incorporating small businesses, and building them into larger ones, and those businesses range from home-based gift baskets and party planning to thriving factories and sprawling high-tech facilities in such fields as the manufacturing of industrial fencing and electronic components.

Rather than feeling helpless when something breaks down, single moms are signing up for classes in small engine repair and deck building, and teaching those skills to their sons. My own sons called me "Tim the Toolman" after the character on the TV show, *Home Improvement*, and they leapt in enthusiastically to help me with the demolition and restoration of our home. Neither they nor any of their friends questioned being taught to install wood flooring by a mom (though an older male neighbor seeing me clearing a field with a brush cutter did stop by to pull a "hey, now, there little lady, you could hurt yourself with that thing" routine. In time, though, even the neighbors got used to seeing me on Saturday morning at the hardware store, and began to offer me the loan of tools from their workshops).

"My son watches as I take out the garbage, mow the lawn, shovel the snow, and so on. I really hope that he learns that men and women can do anything that they set their minds to!"

—*Eileen, single mother of one son*

Single moms are educating themselves about money, making investments decisions, and becoming savvy about retirement plans and mutual funds. They're seeking the input of financial planners and reading books on money management. With that knowledge, more and more are finding ways to achieve home ownership.

Studies have shown that the real risk factors behind most of the problems young sons of single mothers experience are the mother's lack of education and financial hardship. By facing these problems head-on with determination and support, single moms are just as capable of providing the stability and role modeling necessary for the children to succeed as a two-parent household could have.

"I taught my son respect for women. My son opens doors for them. I taught him that. He loves running and trying new sports—I taught him that. We wrestle, play video games together. I've taught him confidence and not to be afraid. He breaks something, to try to fix it. He spills something—clean it up. I'm teaching him about earning money, and different professions. How to help around the house—take out the garbage, make his bed, wash the dishes, clean up his toys. But it's important to forget about perfection and love your son for who and how he is."

—*Angela, single mom*

And finally, single moms are no longer alone in facing their challenges. As society begins to recognize the heavy cost, in dollars and lives and potentials unfulfilled, of impoverished, underemployed and undereducated single mothers, institutions, individuals, and local, state, and federal agencies have all begun to develop programs directed solely for the benefit of single moms.

Programs like the Single Mothers Scholarship Fund, created by the Dallas County Community Colleges Foundation to assist financially needy single mothers to go back to school, even part-time, offer much-needed assistance with the special needs of those women, knowing that the completion of a degree program can boost a single mom into earning a living wage for herself and her family. Western Kentucky University-Glasgow offers the Linda Spear Goad scholarship to provide funds for single moms to attend summer session, when ordinary financial aid is not available, so that they can complete their educations faster. Raise the Nation is an organization devoted to improving the lives of single moms and their families by providing funds for further education, and WISP, the Women's Independence Scholarship Program, helps fund college for women fleeing abusive relationships. Women are helping each other meet the demands of single motherhood with grace, dignity, and optimism.

■ For more information on either Raise the Nation or WISP, please refer to the Educational Resources section of the Appendix.

The most important thing you can do for your son is to maintain a positive attitude about yourself, your son, and your future. Instill in your son the faith and belief that you can both achieve anything you set your minds to. That requires discipline and determination, but know that you are not alone. Build and maintain a supportive network, and access help where you can and need to. Take time to nurture and care for yourself, because it will only be by building up yourself that you can raise up another. Keep the lines of communication open, and be aware of what you're saying, both with your words and with your attitude. Though other people may mentor and support your child, ultimately, his first and most important role model will be you.

As a Mom of a Remarkable Boy, you

- See opportunities, not limitations;
- Never stop striving to better yourself;
- Know that the most important role model your son will ever have is you; and
- Know that your own future, and that of your son, is solely up to you. The future is what you make it!

Useful Web Sites

Single Parent Support Web sites

- ***www.aaasm.org.*** The Web site of the Association of African American Single Mothers. This organization is especially helpful for its Future Leaders Programs, directed at elementary school children, and its emphasis on the special needs of boys of single moms, with their Boys to Men programs.
- ***www.clubmom.com.*** A truly huge Web site with something for everybody. Ask a question to an expert, give advice of your own, chat with other moms, even win rewards for participating.
- ***www.mommymoments.com.*** Free eight-week online parenting course.
- ***www.momsclub.org.*** A support network for stay-at-home moms, whether married or single. Provides a live community support network through its network of local chapters (there are now more than 2,000 chapters with more than 100,000 members). Meetings are held during weekdays and provide babysitting, and there are lots of planned events to bring children to.

- **_www.mops.org._** MOPS stands for Mothers of Preschoolers, and this group reaches out to all moms, whether single or married, working or stay-at-home. MOPS is a Christian-faith-based organization.
- **_www.singlefamilyvoices.com._** Directed both at single moms and single dads, this friendly site is part of the Single Parents Network. Supportive message boards create a sense of community and support, and helpful articles abound.
- **_www.singlemom.com._** Incredibly full Web site with pages and pages of resources for single moms, covering such topics as careers, education, employment, finances, housing, children, and much more. Numerous articles, advice columns, and reviews of books and movies. Whether you're a newly single mom or an old hand at it, this Web site will provide you with a wealth of information and assistance. They also offer a modest "Financial Gifting Program" through which moms dealing with financial hardships can be awarded Wal-Mart gift cards in amounts ranging from $30 to $100.
- **_www.singlemothers.org._** The official site of the National Organization of Single Mothers, Inc., a terrific Web site and a terrific support group.
- **_www.singleparentsnetwork.com._** Linked to other single parent Web sites, Single Parents Network provides articles, chat forums, and a newsletter.
- **_www.usmums.com._** A truly handy site with links to nearly any kind of assistance a single mom might need, ranging from housing, educational financial aid, government aid, and more.

Child Development Information

- **_www.nimh.nih/gov/Publicat/teenbrain.cfm._** Gives a really great overview into adolescent brain development.

Educational Resources

- ***www.adultstudent.com.*** A super useful Web site with testimonials from other returning adult students who have been successful, and tips on skills that might have gotten rusty, like note taking. Also links to info on financial aid and more.

- ***www.edu.programadvisor.com.*** Extremely useful and informative Web site that discusses which career fields are growing, how to select a degree program, how to apply for financial aid, and much, much more.

- ***www.educationfinancepartners.com.*** When federal student aid doesn't cover all your expenses for school, private lenders can fill in the gaps. This Web site has information on private loans available through their member lenders, along with loan applications.

- ***www.fafsa.ed.gov.*** Web site for the federal student financial aid application.

- ***www.FamilyEducation.com.*** Thorough resource for any parent with a school-age child, you'll find links here to valuable resources for helping your child with his schoolwork, including skill-building tips and downloadable help sheets.

- ***www.FurtherYourEducation.com.*** Great for all non-traditional and returning students, this site will offer you guidance to help you decide on an educational and career path that's right for you, and information about how to pursue it.

- ***www.jiskha.com.*** Here's where to go when your child has a question they just can't find the answer to. Jiskha has over 200 experts available to offer homework help and answer questions on nearly any academic subject, ranging from math and social sciences to physical education and foreign languages. The site serves more than 4,000 students a day.

- *www.Math.com.* The solution to the problem of not remembering (and never having learned!) how to do the tricky math problems your son brings home, this site has help with all math topics, so you can brush up on the subject and help your son.

- *www.raisethenation.org.* Raise the Nation recognizes the financial hardship borne by single mothers, and realizes that a good education is the way to earning a livable wage. This organization provides scholarships for single moms and their kids, and also provides funds for the repayment of existing student loans. Applications are available through the Web site. If you're one of the luckier moms who has already completed her education, pass along the gift of a college degree to another mom by donating to Raise the Nation through the site.

- *http://salliemae.collegeanswer.com.* Provides information on the entire process of saving for college, selecting a school, applying for admission, finding out what financial aid is available, and more. Whether you're looking into furthering your own education or planning for your son's, this is a great place to start.

- *http://studentaid.ed.gov.* Download the latest information on federal student aid from the U.S. government in "Funding Education Beyond High School: The Guide to Federal Student Aid."

- *www.sunshineladyfdn.org/wisp.html.* WISP stands for the Women's Independence Scholarship Program, which provides financial scholarships for single mothers who have left abusive partners and need assistance in returning to school to move forward with their lives. They also provide scholarships for the sons and daughters of WISP graduates through their Change Your World Scholarship.

- *www.fastweb.com.* Amazing online resource that will help you pick a school, find a job or internship, and locate any scholarships or grants that match your profile. You can sign up for e-mail notification of new scholarships and grants you should apply for and even reminders as the deadline approaches.

Housing Resources

- *www.coabode.com.* If you're thinking it's cheaper to share a home with a similar-minded single mom, here's the place to get started. Save money and time, and have the support of a partner at home.
- *www.ic.org.* IC stands for intentional community (or what used to be called communes). Explore and see if living in a community that shares its resources and labor in an atmosphere of cooperation and mutual support would be right for you.
- *www.ncsha.org.* The National Council of State Housing Agencies provides information on a number of methods for low-income families to acquire affordable housing. Particularly of interest are Housing Bonds, which are used by state and local governments to finance low-cost mortgages for lower-income, first-time home buyers.

Child Support and Child Support Enforcement

- *www.childsupport-aces.org.* ACES stands for the Association for Children for Enforcement of Support, a child support advocacy group with more than 40,000 members. This is a good place to start if you're have back-owed child support or are having difficulty collecting your child support.
- *www.ncsea.org.* The Web site of the National Child Support Enforcement Association, a group of child support professionals. However, this site also has links for parents, and can be used to locate information and contact your state or local child support enforcement agencies.

- *http://singleparents.about.com/od/legalissues/qt/cs resources.htm.* A terrific Web page listing links to your local state resources. A good place to start your search for support in enforcing child support orders.

Financial Assistance for Single Moms

- *www.govbenefits.gov.* Handy online survey compiles your information and gives you a list of possible benefit programs you may qualify for, along with links to the sites to seek more information and apply.
- *www.government-grants-for-women.* This Web site provides some basic background on what grants can be used for, and has several grant packages available for purchase that provide in-depth information on the full range of available grants, as well as how to apply for each.
- *www.grants.gov.* Run in partnership with the U.S. Department of Health and Human Services, this site helps prospective applicants find and apply for grants.

Career Resources

- *www.CareerWomen.com.* Devoted solely to women. Post your resume, search job listings, contact employers, or post a listing for a job opening you want filled in your own company.
- *www.nawbo.org.* Web site for the National Association of Women Business Owners. Members have access to resources to help bolster their businesses' success.
- *www.score.org.* Web site of the Service Corps of Retired Executives. An invaluable organization to get to know if you're thinking about or planning to launch a small business of your own. The Web site offers online courses, advice, articles on topics of interest to small business owners, and loads of other resources.

- *www.we-inc.org.* The Web site of Women Entrepreneurs, Inc., an association of women business owners whose goal is to help female entrepreneurs succeed.
- *www.womenwork.org.* Web site for women's employment. They help with job counseling, resume writing, placement, skills development, child-care questions, and more. The Career Center of the site assists with decisions on self-employment as well.

Child Care Resources

- *www.acf.hhs.gov/grants/open.html.* Seeking a way to fund new child-care opportunities in your area? This site lists funding available for child-care programs
- *www.aupairsearch.com.* Use this Web site to learn more about au pairs, join in discussions with other parents, and seek an au pair for your family.
- *www.childcareaware.org.* Help with making decisions on child care and links to your local Child Care Resource and Referral agency.
- *www.naccrra.net/MilitaryPrograms.* Helps military moms find and afford child care that suits their needs through a program of subsidies.
- *www.nccic.org.* Web site of the National Child Care Information Center. Links designated for parents can provide information on assistance in finding and paying for child care, as well as articles regarding child-care and early education issues.
- *www.ymca.net.* The Y is the nation's largest provider of day care, as well as after-school programs and camps. Get to know your Y!

Health Resources

- *http://eap.partners.org/WorkLife/Addiction/kids_and_drugs/signs_and_symptoms_of_drug_use.asp.* A comprehensive list to help you determine if your child might be using drugs.
- *www.guidetopsychology.com.* An informative Web site about issues regarding emotional health, with articles on such diverse subjects as how to break bad habits, overcome fears, and choosing a practitioner. There's even information here for students of psychology.
- *www.insurekidsnow.gov.* Use this Web site to locate programs through your state for free or reduced-cost health insurance for your child, or research available programs in states you may be considering moving to. Many states have very generous income guidelines to qualify, and many also provide health insurance for low-income moms, too.
- *www.mediacampaign.org.* The site of the Office of National Drug Control Policy. You can link here to studies and articles as well as ads concerning drug use prevention, trends, the impact of drug use, and more.
- *www.mentalhealth.gov.* This Web site of the National Institute of Mental Health offers information on such mental health issues as ADD/ADHD, autism, eating disorders, and more, along with updates on the latest research and programs that they're funding.
- *www.nmha.org.* The Web site of Mental Health America, this huge online resource provides information on disorders, medication, where and how to get help, and even information on paying for treatment with insurance or Medicaid. Whether you're looking for answers for your child or yourself, this site is a good place to start your search.

- **www.theantidrug.com.** Informative Web site for information on drugs, drug use, and how and where to get help for your child. Stresses drug prevention through parental interaction and awareness.

Athletics Resources

- **www.littleleague.org.** Get more information on the league, find your local league, and get information on baseball camps.
- **www.MomsTeam.com.** Sane, helpful information and advice for any mom with a child involved with sports. The emphasis here is on solutions to problems and situations you might encounter, as well as an interactive element to offer advice, support, and guidance.
- **www.NationalPal.org.** The site of the National Police Athletic/Activities League (PAL), an association that brings kids in contact with police officers in the context of organized sports. PAL chapters are active in most larger towns and cities across the country.

Miscellaneous

- **www.family-reunion.com.** A good starting point when thinking about planning a family reunion. Great ideas and planning suggestions, and a great motivator, too!
- **www.fcc.gov/vchip.** Provides in-depth information on the TV ratings system and the use of the V-chip that TVs are now required to come equipped with.
- **www.legalmomentum.org.** A women's rights advocacy group with the latest information on legal issues of interest and relevance to women.
- **www.nsopr.gov.** This Web site allows access to the National Sex Offenders Registry, which lists registered sex offenders

by community and their listed address, and gives some basic information on the offender's history, such as what type of offense he was convicted of.

- *www.pflag.org.* Complete resource for the family and friends of a gay teen or adult. Find support, education, contact local chapters, and access the latest information.
- *www.yoga.about.com.* This Web site explains in detail the various types of yoga so you can choose the style that will best suit your temperament, physical condition, and fitness goals.

INDEX